Franklin Delano Roosevelt

Roy Jenkins

THE AMERICAN PRESIDENTS
ARTHUR M. SCHLESINGER, JR., GENERAL EDITOR

Completed with the Assistance of Richard E. Neustadt

THORNDIKE
CHIVERS

This Large Print edition is published by Thorndike Press®, Waterville, Maine USA and by BBC Audiobooks, Ltd, Bath, England.

Published in 2004 in the U.S. by arrangement with Henry Holt and Company, LLC.

Published in 2004 in the U.K. by arrangement with Pan Macmillan Ltd.

U.S. Hardcover 0-7862-6292-3 (Biography)
U.K. Hardcover 0-7540-9865-6 (Chivers Large Print)
U.K. Softcover 0-7540-9866-4 (Camden Large Print)

The text of this Large Print edition is unabridged.
Other aspects of the book may vary from the original edition.

Set in 16 pt. Plantin.

Printed in the United States on permanent paper.

British Library Cataloguing-in-Publication Data available

Library of Congress Cataloging-in-Publication Data

Jenkins, Roy, 1920–
    Franklin Delano Roosevelt / Roy Jenkins ; completed with the assistance of Richard Neustadt.
        p. cm.
    Originally published: New York : Times Books, 2003.
    ISBN 0-7862-6292-3 (lg. print : hc : alk. paper)
    1. Roosevelt, Franklin D. (Franklin Delano), 1882–1945.
    2. Presidents — United States — Biography.   3. Large type books.   I. Neustadt, Richard E.   II. Title.
    E807.J46 2003b
    973.917′092—dc22
        [B]   2003070312

Franklin Delano Roosevelt

CONTENTS

Editor's Note

THE AMERICAN PRESIDENCY

The president is the central player in the American political order. That would seem to contradict the intentions of the Founding Fathers. Remembering the horrid example of the British monarchy, they invented a separation of powers in order, as Justice Brandeis later put it, "to preclude the exercise of arbitrary power." Accordingly, they divided the government into three allegedly equal and coordinate branches — the executive, the legislative, and the judiciary.

But a system based on the tripartite separation of powers has an inherent tendency toward inertia and stalemate. One of the three branches must take the initiative if the system is to move. The executive branch alone is structurally capable of taking that initiative. The Founders must have sensed this when they accepted Alexander Hamilton's proposition in the Seventieth Federalist that "energy in the executive is a leading character in the definition of good government." They thus envisaged a strong president — but within an equally strong system of constitutional accountability. (The term *imperial presidency* arose in the 1970s to describe the situation when the balance between power and accountability is upset in favor of the executive.)

The American system of self-government thus comes to focus in the presidency — "the vital place of action in the system," as Woodrow Wilson put it. Henry Adams, himself the great-grandson and grandson of presidents as well as the most brilliant of American historians, said that the American president "resembles the commander of a ship at sea. He must have a helm to grasp, a course to steer, a port to seek." The men in the White House (thus far only men, alas) in steering their chosen courses have shaped our destiny as a nation.

Biography offers an easy education in American history, rendering the past more human, more vivid, more intimate, more accessible, more connected to ourselves. Biography reminds us that presidents are not supermen. They are human beings too, worrying about decisions, attending to wives and children, juggling balls in the air, and putting on their pants one leg at a time. Indeed, as Emerson contended, "There is properly no history; only biography."

Presidents serve us as inspirations, and they also serve us as warnings. They provide bad examples as well as good. The nation, the Supreme Court has said, has "no right to expect that it will always have wise and humane rulers, sincerely attached to the principles of the Constitution. Wicked men, ambitious of power, with hatred of liberty and contempt of law, may fill the place once occupied by Washington and Lincoln."

The men in the White House express the ideals and the values, the frailties and the flaws of the voters who send them there. It is altogether natural that we should want to know more about the virtues and the vices of the fellows we have elected to govern us. As we know more about them, we will know more about ourselves. The French political philosopher Joseph de Maistre said, "Every nation has the government it deserves."

At the start of the twenty-first century, forty-two men have made it to the oval office. (George W. Bush is counted our forty-third president because Grover Cleveland, who served nonconsecutive terms, is counted twice.) Of the parade of presidents, a dozen or so lead the polls periodically conducted by historians and political scientists.

11

What makes a great president?

Great presidents possess, or are possessed by, a vision of an ideal America. Their passion, as they grasp the helm, is to set the ship of state on the right course toward the port they seek. Great presidents also have a deep psychic connection with the needs, anxieties, dreams of people. "I do not believe," said Wilson, "that any man can lead who does not act . . . under the impulse of a profound sympathy with those whom he leads — a sympathy which is insight — an insight which is of the heart rather than of the intellect."

"All of our great presidents," said Franklin D. Roosevelt, "were leaders of thought at a time when certain ideas in the life of the nation had to be clarified." So Washington incarnated the idea of federal union, Jefferson and Jackson the idea of democracy, Lincoln union and freedom, Cleveland rugged honesty. Theodore Roosevelt and Wilson, said FDR, were both "moral leaders, each in his own way and his own time, who used the presidency as a pulpit."

To succeed, presidents must not only have a port to seek but they must convince Congress and the electorate that it is a port worth seeking. Politics in a democracy is ultimately an educational process, an adventure in persuasion and consent. Every president stands in Theodore Roosevelt's bully pulpit.

The greatest presidents in the scholars' rankings, Washington, Lincoln, and Franklin Roosevelt, were leaders who confronted and overcame the republic's greatest crises. Crisis widens presidential opportunities for bold and imaginative action. But it does not guarantee presidential greatness. The crisis of secession did not spur Buchanan or the crisis of depression spur Hoover to creative leadership. Their inadequacies in the face of crisis allowed Lincoln and the second Roosevelt to show the difference individuals make to history. Still, even in the absence of first-order crisis, forceful and persuasive presidents — Jefferson, Jackson, Theodore Roosevelt, Ronald Reagan — are able to impose their own priorities on the country.

The diverse drama of the presidency offers a fascinating set of tales. Biographies of American presidents constitute a chronicle of wisdom and folly, nobility and pettiness, courage and cunning, forthrightness and deceit, quarrel and consensus. The turmoil perennially swirling around the White House illuminates the heart of the American democracy.

It is the aim of the American Presidents series to present the grand panorama of our chief executives in volumes compact enough for the busy reader, lucid enough for the student, authoritative enough for the scholar. Each volume offers a distillation of character and career. I hope that these lives will give readers some understanding of the pitfalls and potentialities of the presidency and also of the responsibilities of citizenship. Truman's famous sign — "The buck stops here" — tells only half the story. Citizens cannot escape the ultimate responsibility. It is in the voting booth, not on the presidential desk, that the buck finally stops.

— Arthur M. Schlesinger, Jr.

A Note on the Text

Shortly before completing the final text of this book, Roy Jenkins suffered a sudden, unexpected fatal heart attack. The space break on page 242 indicates the last words he wrote. At the request of his widow, Dame Jennifer Jenkins, this chapter has been completed by their friend Richard E. Neustadt of Harvard University, with whom Lord Jenkins had intended to discuss it.

1

Roosevelt Cousins

Franklin Delano Roosevelt was the thirty-second president of the United States, and the only one to be elected more than twice. In any rating of presidents there can be no more than three of his predecessors who could be placed in contention with him, and of his successors there are so far none. Although of a provenance grander in the social scale than any of the others except perhaps for George Washington and his own kinsman Theodore Roosevelt, he did not coast to the White House, and soon after he got there aroused unprecedented upper-class hostility. Known as Feather Duster by some of his early contemporaries, he was originally regarded as a lightweight, and his life contained several setbacks and one apparent catastrophe.

He was more tested in peace and war than any president other than Lincoln. Although often seen as a patrician among professional politicians, he was perhaps the most skilled politician of the lot. He was even more than that: he was a blazer of trails. He aroused great loyalty and he dazzled those around him with inspiriting personal charm. Yet by the end of his not very long life several of those who had most helped his rise had moved not only to detachment but to full opposition. He was therefore a man as full of ambiguity as he was of power and interest.

He was protean, and hence very difficult to get hold of. He was a hero who had many unheroic characteristics. He was almost the opposite of the tribute that his companion in arms Winston Churchill paid to his own great friend Lord Birkenhead. "In any affair, public or personal," Churchill wrote, "if he was with you on the Monday, you would find him the same on the Wednesday; and on the Friday, when things looked blue, he would still be marching forwards with strong reinforcements." If Roosevelt was pressing an associate to undertake some controversial assignment on a Monday, it was only too likely that by the Wednesday he would have decided to split the job, or to give it to somebody else instead, and that by the Friday, if things looked blue, he would have moved toward abandoning the project altogether, or at any rate for the time being. Yet he was a man of massive achievement, whom, on balance, it is difficult not greatly to admire.

Equally paradoxically, while he was thought of as a leader with a program — the New Deal has remained resonant in history for over seventy years — he was much more of an improviser than an ideologue. He nudged his way forward. If something did not work, he was always willing to try something else. After three election victories and nearly nine highly controversial years in the White House, he became engaged in the winning of the biggest war in American history, although it is arguable that Lincoln's experience was still more testing because it came nearer to defeat. But what is indisputable is that 1941–45 saw an incomparable mobilization of American effort, industrial and military. In Europe by 1945, the U.S. Army dwarfed the British by three to one, and in the Pacific the preponderance was many times greater. But, above all, it was the massive outpouring of American industrial strength, converted to guns and tanks, aircraft and ships, which became the eighth wonder of the world, and after the relatively short period of three and a half years made victory inevitable over the formidable military machines of Germany and Japan. Roosevelt, who had been so excoriated by business leaders for much of his first and second terms, was able in his third term to preside over this spectacular achievement, even if under a good deal of government direction, of the capitalist-controlled American industrial machine.

Another of Roosevelt's paradoxes was that, although a New Yorker of Dutch family origin and a Hudson Valley squire — in other words, a product not of the heartland but of the extreme eastern edge and most Europe-oriented part of America — he was peculiarly successful at transcending geography and uniting the continent. His strongest support was never on the eastern seaboard. In his landslide victory of 1936, for instance, the only two states that stood against the Republican debacle were Vermont and Maine. And in 1944, which was the last contest and the hardest fought, it was the late-declaring western states that contradicted the equivocation of the early eastern results.

Roosevelt was also an outstanding example of a leader who, although not in any full sense an intellectual (he was a book collector rather than a book reader, and his Harvard grades were of a mediocrity that suggest that today he might have had difficulty in gaining entry to that august institution), had an unusual capacity to inspire the intellectual classes. So did John F. Kennedy, and so, too, did FDR's family predecessor in the presidency, Theodore Roosevelt. But TR, bizarre mixture of frenetic cowboy and New York grandee though he was, had much greater historical knowledge and a higher capacity for literary composition than anything Franklin Roosevelt ever exhibited. Yet any serious assessment would put the President Roosevelt of 1933–45 substantially higher than the President Roosevelt of 1901–1909. They both had long enough presidencies (FDR's of unprecedented length) to qualify for a gold medal. Franklin Roosevelt effortlessly achieves it, but Theodore Roosevelt has to remain content with a silver or perhaps even a bronze.

It is impossible to understand Franklin Roosevelt (difficult enough in any case) without appreciating the influence that his remote cousin had upon the first thirty-eight years of his life. Although their degree of consanguinity (they were fifth cousins) was far less than that of the two Adamses, the two Harrisons, or the two Bushes, the resonance of the Roosevelt name in American history is not only greater than that of the other pairs but is also a joint legacy of both its presidential bearers. Both Theodore and Franklin were eighth-generation Americans, being equally descended from Claes Martenszen van Rosenvelt, who had arrived in New Amsterdam from Haarlem in Holland about twenty years before the change of name to New York in 1664. The two presidents were equally descended from his son Nicholas, American born in 1658. Thereafter the two families split, the elder of Nicholas's two sons founding what became known as the Oyster Bay (Long Island) branch of the family, into which, almost two hundred years later, Theodore was to be born, and the younger producing the Hyde Park (Hudson Valley) branch, which added Franklin twenty-three years after that. The position was complicated by Franklin marrying in 1905 a daughter of the (dead) younger brother of Theodore, who was then in the White House but who nonetheless came to New York and gave a presidential blessing to the wedding. What is indisputable is that both Roosevelt presidents came of impeccable New York stock, with many generations of prosperity behind them. Insofar as there is an American aristocracy (and a very powerful case can be made for its existence) both Roosevelts clearly belonged to it. Indeed the middle stretch of the Hudson Valley, particularly the eastern bank, from just south of Albany through Tivoli, Hyde Park, Poughkeepsie, and Garrison to Peekskill, was laid out in a series of grand squirearchical estates unmatched by any concentration in England or France. They followed one another along the river like fine pearls in a necklace. They made the properties in the so-called dukeries of northwest Nottinghamshire look sporadic. And there the riparian squires lived a pattern of life that was not ostentatious but determinedly gentlemanly.

James Roosevelt (FDR's father) was well described as

a tall man with mutton chops whiskers who was rarely without a riding crop. He bred trotters and built a famous herd of Alderneys that he crossed with Jerseys and Guernseys. He took the cure annually at a German spa, hunted in Pau, shot grouse in Scotland, and as a patriarch was amongst those who decided who belonged to New York society. While declining to take part in politics as not quite gentlemanly, he fulfilled a squire's obligation to the Volunteer Fire Company, was warden and vestryman of the church, and served as town supervisor. And as president of a small railroad company he was entitled to take his private railroad car . . . to any part of the country.

He and those like him were in New York City for the relatively short late fall season, but in general they preferred to spend most of the year in their river residences, perhaps going to the city a day or so a week in order to look after their substantial inherited portfolios, but not to strive too officiously to add to them.

The Oyster Bay Roosevelts were Long Island Sound rather than Hudson River grandees, but they added to the vast cousinage, which was a very self-conscious link not only between the two Roosevelt branches, but also with many of the other old New York families. They used the terms "Cousin X" and "Cousin Y" in a way that similar English families, Cavendishes and Spencers, Cecils and Stanleys, would not have thought of doing. When the very unpretentious Eleanor Roosevelt became engaged to FDR in 1903 and had to write to her formidable mother-in-law-to-be, Sara Roosevelt, she always improbably addressed her as "Cousin Sally." So rampant indeed was the practice that one is reminded of the joke about the Armenian family which claimed to be so old that they always spoke of the Virgin as "Cousin Mary."

Somewhere along the way the two branches of the family had become separated in their politics. The Oyster Bay branch had been Republicans at least since the Civil War, even though they had been true to the New York attitude of leaving perfervid involvement in that conflict to Boston and Philadelphia. The father of TR had bought himself a substitute rather than participate in the Union army — which may be thought a profoundly ironical bit of history in view of the "biff 'em" school, not only of diplomacy but of personal conduct, of which his son was such a notable exponent. Their Republicanism was, however, an affiliation that fitted naturally with their late-nineteenth-century social milieu.

What was more surprising was that the Hyde Park Roosevelts had become loosely Democratic. FDR's father was a supporter of Grover Cleveland, a New Yorker who was himself fairly right wing and was the only man to have two separate terms as president. James Roosevelt was a Democrat because his father had been one, and he liked established habits; his attitude to his party was like that of many old Whigs to the British Liberal party before they split with Gladstone over Home Rule in 1886.

It was in several ways paradoxical that the Hyde Park Roosevelts should have been more unorthodox in their politics than the Oyster Bay ones. Immured in the countryside on their Hudson River bluff, eighty miles upriver (although they were never without a Manhattan residence for occasional use), they were much more detached from the largely Democratic city, both by geography and by involvement, than were their cousins on the much nearer part of Long Island. It pointed more to the absence of any rigid ideological position in American party politics at the time than to any virulence of socioeconomic dispute between the two branches. Not that it was a dull period in American politics. The first dozen years of the twentieth century, culminating in the presidential election of 1912, were some of the most interesting between Lincoln and the second Roosevelt. But the interest was more within and across parties than in any clear clash between two already defined and well-drawn-up armies.

Franklin Roosevelt's relations with his

distant kinsman (and uncle-in-law as he was to become) epitomized this. The two Roosevelts were influenced by much the same impulses. Moreover, Franklin Roosevelt in his early days was imbued with an envy of the life of Oyster Bay, more pulsating than that of Hyde Park. At Oyster Bay, or Sagamore Hill as the house was called, there was almost excessive boisterousness. By 1898 TR had six children, varying in age between fourteen and one, and all of them, when the patriarch was at home, were pushed into a relentless regime of athletic exercise and, maybe, fun. There were also first cousins and nephews and nieces (including Eleanor, born in 1884) intermittently present. The life of Franklin at Springwood, the always pale and now almost forgotten name of the estate at Hyde Park, was by contrast solitary to the point of loneliness. At his birth on January 30, 1882, his father was fifty-three; his only sibling, a half brother known as Rosy Roosevelt, was twenty-seven and far away. His mother, born Sara Delano, who claimed an even grander lineage than the Roosevelts, was a commanding, ever-present, and devoted matriarch who retained this position until 1941, in the ninth year of Franklin Roosevelt's presidency. Although she was one of nine children, her share of her father's legacy was more than a million nineteenth-century dollars. That father, Warren Delano, was responsible for a wonderfully patronizing remark about his daughter's husband, James Roosevelt, FDR's father, who was as upper class as he was elderly. James was "the first person who made me realize that a Democrat can be a gentleman," Delano said. But Sara could not provide much in the way of adolescent friendship. When, therefore, Franklin was invited to spend a July Fourth at Sagamore Hill he was determined to accept, in spite of mild opposition from his parents, and when he got there he found the enthusiastic gregariousness intoxicating.

Apart from the fact that TR never went to school but was privately tutored until he went to Harvard in 1876, the two Roosevelts' lives pursued a remarkably parallel course — at an interval of twenty-three years. And Franklin did not attend school until, at the age of fifteen, he was sent to Groton, the would-be copy of Eton (although in fact its style and appearance were much more like Cheltenham's or Marlborough's) that the Reverend Endicott Peabody had established in northern Massachusetts a dozen years before.

Neither Roosevelt achieved academic distinction, although TR, in spite of his endemic Boy Scoutism, absorbed more historical method and knowledge. He was also more sociably successful, being easily elected to the most fashionable Harvard club, Porcellian, whereas Franklin had to make do with the Fly Club — among the second rank of such bodies. The habits of Porcellian members, always subsequently wearing little pigs as pendants on their watch chains and cabaling together even at the most inappropriate occasions, makes one feel that Franklin may have been lucky to be rejected. And he achieved what might be regarded as the more interesting undergraduate distinction by becoming president (in effect, editor) of the *Crimson*, the Harvard undergraduate newspaper.

Both fathers died during their son's first years at Harvard; Theodore experienced more grief, although maybe Franklin suffered more inconvenience, for the early widowhood of Sara Roosevelt led her to take lodgings in Boston in order to keep a closely maternal eye upon her only son. However, it is after Harvard that the similarity in the careers of the two cousins really shows. TR, after being elected a New York State assemblyman at the age of twenty-three and making a humiliatingly unsuccessful bid for the mayoralty of New York in 1886, convalesced first as a civil service commissioner in Washington under the presidency of Benjamin Harrison and then, more flamboyantly, as president of the New York City Board of Police Commissioners before becoming assistant secretary of the navy in the McKinley administration in 1897. After a relatively brief spell there, TR resigned in order to get himself appointed to a military command in the Spanish-American War. In Cuba, as a colonel, he led his amateur battalion of "Rough Riders" in a cavalry charge up the hill of San Juan and gave himself an immense national fame.

At this stage it is not so much the future career of Franklin Roosevelt as the contemporary activities of Winston Churchill that TR's parabola calls to mind. Churchill, a lieutenant of hussars, had received his baptism of fire on that same island of Cuba during an earlier 1895 imbroglio and had then participated and written books about, successively, a punitive expedition on the North-West Frontier of India and one of the last cavalry charges in British military history, at Omdurman in the Sudan in 1898. Then, in 1899, he had rushed out to the war in South Africa, where he escaped from a brief incarceration in a prisoner-of-war compound. And he had used the fame so acquired to get himself elected to Parliament at the age of twenty-five in 1900. TR did not like what he heard and read about the brashness of the young Churchill, which enabled his daughter, Alice Roosevelt Longworth, to score a bull's-eye by telling Arthur Schlesinger, many years later, that this was because her father and Churchill "were so alike."

In 1898, TR used his fame to be elected (even if only narrowly) governor of New York State at the age of forty. The executive mansion at Albany, as the examples of Martin Van Buren and Grover Cleveland before him and Charles Evans Hughes, Al Smith, Franklin Roosevelt, and Thomas Dewey after him showed, was regarded as a fine stepping-stone to at least a presidential candidature. TR, however, had to make do with a vice presidential position on the 1900 Republican ticket, with McKinley, the incumbent and a former governor of Ohio, in the top spot. But within ten months of McKinley's reelection Theodore Roosevelt was president by assassination.

Franklin Roosevelt, in a mixture of emulation and contrast, became a Democratic state senator in 1910 at the age of twenty-eight but — unusually for a Democrat — for his own county of Dutchess and a couple of those adjacent. Theodore, twenty-eight years before, had been elected by a New York City constituency, admittedly about the most upper-crust one, then known as the Brownstone District, later to be rechristened, as it shifted uptown, the Silk Stocking District. In 1913, having once won reelection, Franklin Roosevelt was appointed assistant secretary of the navy in the new Woodrow Wilson administration. He stayed in that post much longer than TR had done, although balancing that longer Washington period by an attempt to rise higher in New York elective positions that was as misjudged as had been TR's mayoralty bid in 1886. In August 1914, when Armageddon was engulfing Europe and it might have been thought that the warrior chief of World War II would have his mind concentrated on the need to strengthen the U.S. Navy (which at that stage was no more than half the size, or at any rate received only half the budgetary support, of Winston Churchill's Royal Navy), he devoted himself to a primary contest for the New York Democratic nomination for the U.S. Senate. He was soundly beaten by James W. Gerard, Wilson's ambassador in Berlin, who ought also to have had other things on his mind at the time. The crowning irony was that Gerard was then defeated by the Republican candidate in the general election. It was Franklin Roosevelt's only electoral defeat, apart from sharing in the Democratic loss of 1920, but a fairly humiliating one, born out of bad judgment and restless ambition.

He then returned to his Navy Department desk and remained nominally there until the sad end of the Wilson administration in 1921, the president himself and his policies being equally crippled. He had a good deal of power in his theoretically junior job, for his Cabinet superior, Josephus Daniels, was a pacifically minded southern newspaper editor. Daniels liked Roosevelt, although miles away from him in his view of world politics as well as socially, and was happy to let him get on with things in the department.

This Roosevelt did with reasonable success, although he got dragged down by a very messy naval drugs and homosexual scandal at Newport, Rhode Island, in 1919–20. There was no question of FDR being personally involved in the debauchery, if that is what it was. Homosexuality was never among his temptations. But he seems to have condoned the setting up and use of an agent provocateur special investigative section, which, following intervention by Daniels and a Senate inquiry, was closed down, with Roosevelt being mildly censured. His actions were described as "unfortunate and ill-advised." The episode cast a shadow over him, but a surprisingly light one. He had not come out of it well, revealing an initial lack of judgment and subsequently attempting a clumsy cover-up. Yet there was remarkably little follow-through or ripple effect. It was a fairly early example of Franklin Roosevelt's "Teflon" quality, a rare and valuable attribute for a politician.

During the war itself, FDR was urged by TR to follow his own example of 1898 and get out of his semicivilian job and into uniform. FDR made an attempt to do this, but not perhaps with quite the fanatical enthusiasm that TR had shown previously and was showing again in 1917 when, at the age of fifty-eight, he badgered Wilson to give him a colonel's command in France. (In this he again struck a parallel with Winston Churchill, who took a sojourn in the trenches in 1915–16.) Wilson turned down both the Roosevelts, which in the case of FDR was only sensible. It would hardly have been right to allow him to exchange the auxiliary administration of a whole service for a junior officer's commission. Nevertheless, the president's refusal left a certain trauma on Franklin Roosevelt. He made two trips to Europe in his assistant secretary's capacity — one from July to September 1918, when the war was still on, and another, accompanied by his wife, in January–February 1919, in the early weeks of the peace. On the first he had seen something of the battlefields when they were still active, and on the second perhaps even more of them as relics.

Subsequently — particularly when, on the eves of his two reelection campaigns of 1936 and 1940, he was very hesitantly, one step forward one step backward, nudging the United States toward greater international commitment, but not to a degree likely to endanger his voting strength — he was inclined to exaggerate his direct knowledge of battlefields and consequent hatred of war. Thus, in the summer of 1936, soon after the outbreak of the Spanish Civil War, he said in a much-publicized and long-remembered speech at Chautauqua in western New York State: "I have seen war. I have seen war on land and sea. I have seen blood running from the wounded. I have seen men coughing out their gassed lungs. I have seen them dead in the mud. I have seen cities destroyed. . . ." Three years later, he went still further when he told a group of senators whom he had to the White House that "he had probably seen more of the [first world] war in Europe than any other living persons." He claimed to have seen more of the battlefields, not only in France and Belgium but in Italy too, than is borne out by any hard survey of his engagement diaries. This may have been partly due to a Theodore Roosevelt-initiated feeling that he ought to have been a fighting soldier or sailor in 1917–18.

It is certainly the case that during his early career FDR was enormously influenced, and even inspired, by his much more famous kinsman. This was across the gulf of party, but party loyalties never sat too heavily on either Roosevelt. Each would sometimes make tactical obeisance to party machines when he thought it necessary to achieve the political advancement that he wanted. But both essentially regarded parties as agents — serving their purposes, occasionally useful but never loved, and to be defied and even discarded if they did not so serve. They certainly never elevated political parties into tribal deities deserving of reverential worship. In this respect, too, there were parallels with Winston Churchill. Yet there were also discrepancies between the Roosevelts. Theodore on the whole played the Republican party machine less skillfully than Franklin did the Democratic one. TR's Bull Moose defection in 1912 brought about the only interruption to Republican domination of national politics from 1896 to 1932, while FDR bequeathed an intact electoral coalition that made the Democrats the dominant force in American politics for a generation after his death.

Nevertheless, in Franklin's young days the admiration and emulation were all one way, as was no doubt natural across an age gap of nearly a quarter century. FDR first came into semi-adult contact with TR in the summer of 1897, when he went to stay at Sagamore Hill and then listened to him give a riveting and hilarious talk at Groton School about his experiences heading the New York City Board of Police Commissioners. A couple of years later, FDR went to Harvard and began consciously to imitate some of TR's props and mannerisms.

He adopted pince-nez spectacles and two of the older politician's favorite words — "*dee*lighted," with a strong long "e" on the first syllable, and "bully," in the sense of good or superior, as in TR's famous later aphorism that the White House was "a bully pulpit." But this was all done in a very superior manner. Franklin Roosevelt was far, at that stage, from having the common touch. He had a finer appearance and, eventually, a much more resonant voice than TR, but as a young man he lacked Theodore's air of concentrated energy. Nevertheless, TR's progressive attitude toward the arrogance of big business and of the social elite made a strong appeal to FDR at that time. Their approach to politics may have been patrician, in the sense that Churchill in his Liberal period was strongly in favor of the underdog provided that he, socially at least, could remain top dog; but FDR liked TR's social concern and was not put off by his aggressive jingoism. Both of them had more faith in the established aristocratic families than in the new breed of rapacious capitalists whose wealth was vaulting over the old money that was used to dominating New York society.

In 1901, Theodore Roosevelt's political career took off. Within little over a year he moved from being the vice presidential candidate to being the new young president, at forty-two the youngest ever to occupy the office. No one rivaled him in this respect until John Kennedy entered the White House sixty years later just short of forty-four.

Not everyone was enthusiastic about this accession of youth to the highest corridors of power. "Now look," said Mark Hanna, the national chairman of the Republican party, who at the end of the nineteenth century had come to epitomize the sacred or profane union of Lincoln's Grand Old Party of emancipation with the leaders of American capitalism at their flood tide, "that damned cowboy is President of the United States." William Allen White, the distinguished Kansas newspaper editor who was a friend (although not always a reliable supporter) of both Roosevelts for over forty years, struck an equally memorable note when he said that "Teddy was reform in a derby, the gayest, cockiest, most fashionable derby that you ever saw." James MacGregor Burns's comment on this was "Some reformers saw it as more of a silk hat."

During the seven and a half years of TR's presidency, Franklin Roosevelt had little difficulty in supporting him, even to some extent identifying with him. In the 1904 presidential election he unhesitatingly voted for him against the staidly conservative and quickly forgotten Democratic candidate, Judge Alton B. Parker. Thirty-four years later he explained with typical jauntiness how his first vote had crossed party lines: "I voted for the Republican candidate . . . because I felt he was a better Democrat than the Democratic candidate." And when he became engaged (at first semisecretly) to the daughter of TR's dead brother in October 1903, and then married her in March 1905, there was far less reluctance on the Oyster Bay side of the family than from Franklin's own mother. TR, in the fourth year of his presidency, not only offered the White House for the ceremony, but when they stuck to their original plan of being married in a (large) cousinly house on New York's Upper East Side he came up from Washington, gave the bride away, and welcomed all the guests. "There's nothing like keeping the name in the family," he told Franklin a little complacently. The choice for performing the actual ceremony, before a temporary altar in the doubtfully sacerdotal atmosphere of two adjacent Seventy-sixth

Street houses, was inevitably the rector of Groton, Endicott Peabody, who sent the couple off into their forty years of marriage with all the certainties of muscular Christianity booming in their ears.

What was perhaps more surprising was that when TR, having unnecessarily withdrawn from seeking a second elected term in 1908, came bounding back onto the political scene in 1912, FDR no longer supported him. It was surprising because TR's 1912 venture, based essentially on his disillusionment with the unexciting conservatism of his chosen Republican successor, William Howard Taft, came the nearest to success of all twentieth-century attempts to break the rigid grip of the American two-party system. TR nearly secured the nomination at the July Republican convention in Chicago. He lost to Taft, who was doggedly supported by the machine, by only 70 votes, although the contested primaries indicated that he was way ahead in popular support. He had undertaken to accept the verdict of the convention, but the heady atmosphere generated by his supporters swept him along. Within a month he had made his break and held his own rebel convention, attended by a thousand delegates, at which a new party was launched. It was officially the National Progressive party, but more commonly called the Bull Moose party, after a famous TR comparison between his own vigor and that ruminant specimen. And it was to contest the November election, with the ex-president as its candidate.

As is normal when a dam of political frustration breaks, there were scenes of great enthusiasm at the launch of the new party. And many people of high quality and loose political affiliation were much attracted by it. Some thought it had too many generals, more than a sufficiency of captains, and even an adequacy of sergeants, but not nearly enough enlisted men. For the present author it carries an irresistible whiff of the early days of the British Social Democratic party in 1981–82. Furthermore, it adopted a platform almost tailor made to suit Franklin Roosevelt. Its appeal was reformist, centrist, and anti–machine politics: pro conservation, female suffrage, and labor's right to organize, but not putting union loyalty or sectional advantage above the national interest. The arrogance of capitalism must be curbed. A graduated income tax and a still more strongly graduated inheritance tax should be introduced. High judicial decisions were often so politically prejudiced against social justice that they should be subject to popular review by referendum (this position anticipated some substantial part of Franklin Roosevelt's 1937 onslaught on the Supreme Court). In general, TR summed up his campaign as being that for "a Square Deal" for the whole American people, a phrase that should again have had anticipatory resonance for FDR.

Yet he gave no support. Since 1910 he had been the Democratic state senator from the area surrounding Hyde Park, by no means natural Democratic territory. He had unexpectedly scraped home in his first election but had strengthened his position when he came up for reelection two years later. Although his first action of any note at Albany had been to oppose the Tammany Hall choice for U.S. senator (senators were still voted for by the state legislature rather than directly elected), he had begun to row back and after a year or so was anxious to repair his bridges with the machine. In any event it would have been more difficult for him, as an elected Democrat, to cast a cross-party vote than it had been when he was a private citizen in 1904. Furthermore, he was becoming enthusiastic about the prospect that

Woodrow Wilson, then governor of New Jersey, might win the Democratic presidential nomination and thereafter the presidential election.

FDR was never to be as personally excited by Wilson as he had been by TR, nor was he as socially close to the chillier and more parsonical personality of that Princeton academic. But in 1912 Wilson had something of the same "social reform and lifter of politics out of the squalor of the smoked filled rooms" appeal. He also looked more likely to win, and FDR was already casting ambitious eyes on the chance of exchanging Albany for Washington and a part in the new administration. Although he was kept off the New York delegation to the Baltimore Democratic National Convention — Tammany was backing the more conservative Champ Clark of Missouri, Speaker of the House, for the nomination — Franklin Roosevelt nonetheless busied himself around the convention hall canvassing hard for Wilson. He summed up his thirty-year-old enthusiasm and his imprecise hopes for the future in a July 2 telegram he sent from Baltimore to his wife, who was with their children in Maine: "Wilson nominated this afternoon all my plans vague splendid triumph."

Uncle Ted — as, since the 1905 marriage,

44

TR had been increasingly often called in the Franklin and Eleanor household — was left to fend for himself. This he did with considerable if not decisive success. He polled 4.1 million votes, pushing Taft, not only the official Republican candidate but the incumbent president, into a humiliating third place, and leaving Wilson, with 6.3 million votes, to canter home with a landslide in the electoral college but only 43 percent of popular support. Nonetheless, Wilson was president, the first Democrat to be so for sixteen years, and had also achieved majorities in both houses of Congress. So FDR's realistic prediction of the likely outcome had been vindicated, as was his hope that this might lead to a Washington post for himself. When he became assistant secretary of the navy in March 1913 (and, as such, the secretary's sole deputy), his pleasure was greatly increased by the thought that it was the same post as that to which Uncle Ted had been appointed in 1897, and that he was nine years younger in achieving it. There was, however, some irony in the thought that he got it only as a result of having "betrayed" Uncle Ted. And it was a betrayal which there are indications that both his wife and his mother — rarely in agreement, particularly against him — had been reluctant to see him commit.

Insofar as there was Sagamore Hill resentment at the apostasy (and there undoubtedly was some, although not so deep as permanently to impair personal relations), it should have been canceled out four years later when Theodore Roosevelt himself staged a much bigger letdown. The National Progressive party wanted TR to lead it in another bid for the presidency. But TR decided that the time for such dreams was past. He rallied to the GOP, maybe a quarter hoping that they might forgive 1912 and give him the nomination. When they gave it to Supreme Court Justice Charles Evans Hughes instead, he swallowed the insult and endorsed Hughes, who only just lost to Wilson. When TR's telegram refusing the nomination was read out to the second and last Progressive party convention, many of the political neophytes whom he had led into politics shed tears of chagrin. He had killed his four-year-old child.

Maybe the lesson of these two incidents is that the politics of party loyalty from time to time makes monkeys of all who accept it. But this has to be balanced by the fact that in democracies those who never accept it are left flapping their wings in impotence. A degree, not too much, of tactical opportunism is essential to the achievement of real power and influence. And nowhere is this truth more vividly illustrated than in the half-similar and half-contrasting careers of the two Roosevelts. The roller coaster ended up more favorably for FDR than for TR.

2

Portrait of a Marriage
That Became Crippled

Before plunging deep into the impact upon Franklin Roosevelt of his first Washington period, which lasted a full seven years (1913–20), it is necessary to go back, not to the ample celebration of his wedding, already dealt with, but to the extraordinary nature of his marriage, which, for a mixture of good and ill, was a salient feature of his life. Eleanor Roosevelt, two and a half years younger than Franklin, came of almost exactly the same social milieu as her husband, a fact underlined by their bearing the same surname and being of one of the old "Knickerbocker" families of New York. That word has survived as the name of a Fifth Avenue club and a popular basketball team. At the time of both their births and upbringings it was a label with as precise a connotation as Whig cousinage in the London of the period, or the Faubourg St.-Germain in the Paris of Proust, or the *nomenklatura* in the Russia of Brezhnev. It did not necessarily imply great wealth, but rather high (mostly secure) prosperity, and an inclination to feel at home only with the limited number of people who accepted the same standards of manners (mostly good) and judgment (mostly narrowly complacent).

Yet in many other ways Franklin and Eleanor were about as different and, as time went on, personally incongruous but publicly sustaining as it is possible easily to imagine. Franklin became the dominating president of the twentieth century, maybe of the whole two hundred and fifteen years of the Republic, and during his uniquely long presidency the United States became the most influential power in the world. Eleanor became the most independent and respected of all the presidential consorts. Dolly Madison may have given a sort of "Congress dancing" glitter to the early White House. Edith Wilson may have exercised unprecedented executive power during the last eighteen months of her husband's tenure. Jacqueline Kennedy may have been an icon of style who illuminated the lives of many friends. Lady Bird Johnson may have done a lot for conservation. Hillary Clinton may have achieved higher elected office than any previous first lady had ever contemplated. But no one competed with Eleanor in the force of her views, in her willingness publicly to express these in a way that was on the whole helpful to FDR's presidency, but by no means invariably so, or in her ability for nearly three decades after her husband's death to carry a torch for Rooseveltian liberalism (with a supercharge added by herself) that resonated throughout the world.

Few things seemed less likely at the time of that East Seventy-sixth Street wedding ceremony. Eleanor Roosevelt had experienced a difficult upbringing for a child born into her privileged world. Her mother was a pretty, conventional, unloving woman who died in 1892, at the age of twenty-nine (when Eleanor was eight), of a cumulative combination of illnesses, with a lack of desire to go on living probably providing the connecting cord. Eleanor never liked her mother, who thought her an unattractive and overserious little girl, disparagingly calling her Granny. The child compensated by doting upon her father, who had been separated from her mother since 1891. Elliott Roosevelt was a charming, hopeless, and totally irresponsible alcoholic, who in turn died in 1894.

Eleanor and a surviving younger brother (another had also died) were then taken in hand by their maternal grandmother, another Hudson Valley matriarch, with a riverside estate at Tivoli, twenty miles upstream from Hyde Park, and of course an Upper East Side residence in New York City. In this ambience Eleanor suffered from an Ugly Duckling syndrome, for the household comprised three younger sisters of her dead mother, all of whom were well-known flirtatious beauties whose minds were far more occupied with beaux than with their own education or the troubles of the world. As if to exacerbate her memories there were also two of her mother's younger brothers, both of whom had a strong propensity to alcoholism. (A puritanical repugnance for alcoholic indulgence, to which her own younger brother also became prey, was in consequence one of her obstacles to providing relaxed companionship for her husband in later life — and even more, although the need for this arose only infrequently, to being an indulgent hostess to Winston Churchill.) And, as if to add a twist of lemon peel to the already overpowering cocktail, there was the occasional presence of her first cousin and almost exact contemporary on her father's side, Alice

Roosevelt, later Longworth, who into her nineties retained a wonderfully sharp tongue, and who essentially regarded Eleanor as a dull little do-gooder.

At the age of fifteen, the "do-gooder" escaped from this *House of Mirth* atmosphere to an English school. Allenswood was something between a finishing school and a proper educational establishment, in a large Victorian house at Wimbledon, seven miles south of the center of London. It catered for about forty girls in their late teens. Eleanor stayed there for three years, and it appears to have done her a world of good. She became a distinct favorite of the seventy-year-old headmistress, Marie Souvestre, who in spite of devoting her life to the education of upper-class young women of several nationalities was essentially a radical freethinker, an avowed atheist, a pro-Boer in the South African War, a disciple of Frederic Harrison and the English Positivists, and a friendly acquaintance of Beatrice Webb. Before Wimbledon she had run a school at Fontainebleau, and at one or the other of the two establishments she had educated a wide variety of young ladies, including one of Eleanor's aunts, the sister of Lytton Strachey, Joseph Chamberlain's two daughters (to whom his sons, Austen and Neville, wrote so devotedly throughout their long political careers), and a German *Gräfin* (a particular friend of Eleanor's) who vigorously defended the kaiser to her in 1915 and was to be still more captivated by Hitler, at least until 1939. Mlle. Souvestre regarded Eleanor as possessing a good mind and being an excellent influence in the school. She adopted a somewhat discriminatory habit, as the girls filed past her to say good night, of kissing some while extending only a handshake to others. Eleanor always got a particularly warm embrace. She was also taken by Mlle. Souvestre on holiday visits to Paris, Florence, and Rome. Altogether the Allenswood experience did a great deal not only for Eleanor's happiness while she was there but also for her self-confidence when she returned to America in the summer of 1902.

Nevertheless she was surprised, flattered, and increasingly bowled over when, within a few months, her debonair and more sophisticated distant cousin Franklin began to show first a strong friendship and then a romantic interest in her. This started on a Hudson River train in the summer of her return, gathered momentum over the following winter season in New York, and led to their secret engagement in the following autumn (of 1903). It was secret — and remained so — for a year because of the opposition of the formidable Sara Roosevelt. Her objection, couched in terms of their being too young, was not so much *ad feminam*, although she never over the remaining thirty-eight years of her life learned to treat Eleanor with much respect, but was essentially based on her jealousy of having to share Franklin with anyone. Since the death of her husband she had become an obsessive mother. There was, however, something in her "youthfulness" point. Eleanor was just nineteen and Franklin only twenty-one, still in his final year at Harvard, with no clear occupational bent and not even started at Columbia Law School, which was to give him a somewhat sketchy legal qualification. Sara applied herself with excessive dedication to giving the young couple opportunities to get over each other. In the late winter of 1904 she took Franklin, together with a Harvard classmate but certainly not Eleanor, on a five-week Caribbean cruise. And no sooner had they got back than she took him to call on Joseph Choate, TR's ambassador in London who was temporarily home, in the unavailing hope that he might provide Franklin with a diplomatic berth three thousand miles away.

She would have sought in vain for any help from the president himself, who, when he heard of the match eight months later, was strongly in favor. He liked Franklin, was probably relieved at the prospect of settling Eleanor, who with the alcoholism of her father and of two of her Hall uncles might have been regarded as having "bad blood," and in principle favored a reknitting of the family. The Halls were also in favor, although sorry to lose Eleanor from Tivoli, where she had become a benevolent piece of cement in an increasingly unstable family. In any event, it was clear that at this stage the determination of Franklin and Eleanor was complete. If Franklin could stand up to his mother on the issue, his resolve was indisputable. Eleanor was deeply romantically in love, although she did not lose her lifelong seriousness. Her letters of the time to him survive (his to her were destroyed by her, probably in 1937, when having gone through them for her first volume of autobiography she found them too poignant for recall) and are shot through not only with overwhelming love but with "grandmotherly" concern (a word of his, too near the bone of her childhood sobriquet for comfort) for his health, his work, his aspirations. To her romantic aspirations there were no limits, as emerged in the Elizabeth Barrett Browning poem that she apparently recited to Franklin at the time of his proposal of marriage, and then wrote out for him in a letter two days later.

Unless you can swear, "For life,
    for death!" —
Oh, fear to call it loving!

Unless you can muse in a crowd all day
On the absent face that fixed you:
Unless you can love, as the angels may,
With the breadth of heaven betwixt you;

Unless you can dream that his faith is fast,
Though behoving and unbehoving;
Unless you can die when the dream
    is past —
Oh, never call it loving!

This moving poem, apart from its clumsy line third from the end, was and remained her credo for partnership between woman and man. It was not fortified by any capacity for physical as well as romantic passion. Whether she ever experienced any intense heterosexual desire, even at the height of her commitment to Franklin, remains very doubtful. But the fact that Franklin did not live up to her credo inflicted a great emotional wound, although it did not diminish her resolve for public partnership, and probably accounted both for her destroying his letters nearly thirty-five years after they were written, and for her resort, in the 1930s and 1940s, to several very close female relationships.

There remains the question of why, in the early 1900s, Franklin was so determinedly taken with Eleanor. It would be a mistake to think that she was without physical appeal in her debutante years. She had grace of figure and movement. She had beautiful hair, well arranged, and, it was said, gravely exquisite manners, which conduced to a quiet appeal to nonpredatory older men. And she had a foal-like innocence, although informed through her eyes and conversation with intelligence and wide interests, which could set alight a beam in a minority of younger men. Despite her greatest deficiency, which was a weak sense of humor, she had several eligible suitors other than Franklin. But it was Franklin she wanted, and the more interesting question is why Franklin — at that stage, in the eyes of some observers, a rather lightweight Prince Charming — wanted her. Joseph Lash, in his masterly 1971 study of their relationship (*Eleanor and Franklin*), answers the question with a directness that gains conviction from verging on the naïve: "Grandmotherly!" he wrote, referring back to the exchange of November 1903. "Do Prince Charmings fall in love with 'grandmotherly' young ladies? Yes, if under the gay surface the prince harbors large ambitions that require a helpmate rather than a playfellow to bring them to fruition."

In the years immediately following their marriage, Eleanor remained a fairly conventional upper-class New York young matron. Between 1906 and 1916 she produced six children, of whom five, one girl and four boys, survived. The exception was the first Franklin Delano Roosevelt, Jr., born in 1909, living only seven months and then replaced, with Elliott Roosevelt intervening, by another son of the same name in 1914. During this decade of pregnancies she was persuaded by a combination of her mother-in-law and an aunt that she ought to give up settlement work, to which she had taken enthusiastically on her return from England, because it might introduce proletarian diseases into her young family. And she is even on record as making a few of the anti-Jewish remarks that were the stock-in-trade of WASP New York society at the time.

Of more significance was the degree of residential subordination she had to accept from Sara Roosevelt — no longer Cousin Sally, as Eleanor had at first insouciantly addressed her, but Mama, as had become her more authoritative designation after the marriage. Hyde Park remained overwhelmingly Sara Roosevelt's domain. Until her death in 1941, Sara Roosevelt always sat at one end of the table, with Franklin at the other end and Eleanor floating indeterminately at one of the sides. Still more symbolic was the arrangement of the bedrooms. The home team was at the south end of the mansion. Franklin had the best bedroom, in the southwest corner, closest to the commanding prospect over the Hudson. Sara had a room of equal size but slightly inferior view in the southeast corner. Eleanor had an austere cell between the two.

When I first saw Hyde Park (over forty years ago), the bedroom hierarchy was one of the two things that most imprinted themselves upon my mind. The other was the self-confidence of the modest arrangements the Roosevelts had made for the visit of the British king and queen in June 1939. They were put up in the normal guest quarters, with two bedrooms, but with conditions made somewhat hugger-mugger by Mackenzie King, the prime minister of Canada, being also in the house at the time and with the layout strongly suggesting that had King George wished to go to the bathroom during the night he would have had to make his way through the prime minister's room. Most subsequent presidents — certainly Johnson, Nixon, and Reagan — would have arranged more lavish outside accommodation, which indeed would have been easily available to the Roosevelts: the far more ornate Vanderbilt mansion was only a couple of miles away, and untenanted at the time. But the Roosevelts were firmly of the view that what was good enough for Hudson Valley gentry should also be good enough for any crowned head. And Sara must have been a full party to this decision, for she maintained complete control over the running of the Hyde Park household until her death two years later, as is epitomized by the official photograph of the visit, which shows her seated complacently in the center, flanked by the king and Eleanor on her right and the queen and Franklin on her left.

Nor did Eleanor easily escape this matriarchal control even when away from Hyde Park. At first, the young married couple did have a house of their own in New York City, on East Thirty-sixth Street, although it had been furnished and the servants engaged by Sara while they were away on an extended European honeymoon. After the two oldest children, Anna and James, had arrived, it was thought that somewhere larger was needed (perhaps also that the tide of fashion uptown should be followed) and a plan was put in hand in 1908 for building a new house at 49 East Sixty-fifth Street. But there was not to be just one house. There were to be two adjacent ones with connecting doors on several floors, and Sara Roosevelt was to occupy the second one. The holiday house at Campobello, on the edge of Maine and New Brunswick, had been equally under Sara's single command for the first four summers of the marriage, but her grip was somewhat relaxed in 1909, when the Franklins acquired a separate cottage. A neighbor who had sympathized with Eleanor's plight bequeathed it to them in her will.

The essential trouble was threefold. First, Eleanor at this stage was submissive and Sara was determinedly dominant. Their relationship is well captured (as is Eleanor's foal-like quality) in a picture of them together in 1904. Second, Franklin had a great capacity, which he was to exhibit frequently in his years of power, for blandly ignoring situations of conflict and difficulty on which he did not want to pronounce. And third, Sara Roosevelt effectively controlled the purse strings. The young Roosevelts had between them an annual income of $12,500, the rough equivalent of perhaps $300,000 today. It was enough, even though Franklin's earned income as a very junior and amateurish lawyer in the white-shoe firm of Carter, Ledyard & Milburn added little, for them to rub along as cadet members of upper-class society. But when anything special was required — a house, a motorcar (Franklin acquired one as early as 1908), a European holiday, school fees when they came along, the doling out of generous (but not unconditional) subventions from Sara Roosevelt was essential.

From the beginning of Franklin's political career, first tentatively as a state senator in 1910 and then plunging in deeper as a junior Cabinet officer in early 1913, he was provided with a purpose and Eleanor with an approach to liberation. Washington was outside the reach of Sara Roosevelt. To her, as to many other great New York ladies of her period, it was an unknown town built on a southern swamp in which the vulgar arts of politics were practiced. This, of course, gave it a considerable appeal to Eleanor, who began to extend her wings, in spite of her six years there being considerably encumbered by pregnancy and young children, even if with plenty of nursery assistance.

Franklin bounded into his new responsibilities with all the enthusiasm of a large, well-bred, full-grown, but only half-trained puppy. He did not have much contact with the president (junior ministers in any country can expect to see little of their head of government), but he became a leading figure in the upper-middle-rank administrative and diplomatic life of a capital responding to all the excitement of a change of political direction after a long period (sixteen years) of one-party rule. With his head of department, Josephus Daniels, he maintained, against the odds, remarkably good relations — as is illustrated in another photograph, that of

63

Daniels participating in a launch party for Roosevelt's vice presidential bid of 1920. The credit for these good relations rests squarely upon Daniels. He was not a great man, but he was an unusually unjealous one.

Daniels was a homespun North Carolina country editor whose father had been a shipwright.* Daniels was aware that he had been assigned an assistant of much greater potential than his own, but behaved with gentlemanly tolerance. This was partly for the simple but good reason that he genuinely liked Roosevelt and was more captivated by his charm and dash than he was put off by his presumption. They agreed on practically no matter of foreign policy, but they both embraced Wilson's liberal democratic ideals. Twenty years later, FDR sent his old boss to carry out the Good Neighbor policy as ambassador to Mexico, one of his most successful diplomatic appointments. Daniels, in the Wilson

---

*This was his only and somewhat tenuous connection with nautical matters. Otherwise he recalled the satirical jingle about the more portentous G. J. Goschen when the latter became British First Lord of the Admiralty in 1895: "Goschen has no notion of the ocean."

Cabinet, was the junior partner of William Jennings Bryan, three times the unsuccessful Democratic candidate for the presidency, who had joined as secretary of state. Together they represented the populist, noneastern wing of Wilson's support, and as such were very important to him. They were also the pacifist wing, which after the beginning of the European war in August 1914 became the neutralist wing. Bryan indeed resigned as early as June 1915 because he thought Wilson was showing too much sympathy for France and Britain.

This resignation made Daniels the more politically valuable to Wilson, although not navally so. Until well into the second year of the European war, Daniels saw his main duty as avoiding too large a U.S. Navy, and as providing a good further education rather than battle training for its 65,000 personnel (including the Marine Corps). It was nonetheless already the third navy in the world (after only the British and the French), although markedly weaker in the aggressive weapon of the submarine than was the German. Daniels's longest-lasting impact upon the American navy was to make it dry in the spring of 1914, which was no obvious contribution to the fostering of offensive spirit.

As Atlantic sinkings increased and the United States edged toward war, Daniels's pacifist spirit strengthened Roosevelt's hand both with the president and within the Navy Department. From 1914, Roosevelt was strongly in favor of the allies. And long before April 1917, egged on by Uncle Ted (who had put behind him FDR's apostasy of 1912 and had resurfaced in a bellicose mood), he grew increasingly impatient for American intervention. Daniels was quite prepared to let FDR get on with it. His pacifism had become theoretical. Provided he himself did not have to make too many recanting statements he was content to let his subordinate prepare the department for war. Roosevelt was allowed not merely to organize the dockyards, which was the assistant secretary's traditional sphere of activities, but also to develop a much closer strategic relationship with the admirals than was usual. He also made a habit, at least according to his own account, of using the fairly frequent periods when Daniels was away from Washington to clear up the papers languishing upon his desk and to make many bellicose decisions, which were not subsequently repudiated.

In Washington, the Roosevelts lived at 1733 N Street, a hundred-year-old residence in the heart of Georgetown, which, however, had not then acquired its fashionable patina of the second half of the twentieth century. This was to some extent an escape for Eleanor, but not a complete one from the family, for the house belonged to her aunt Bamie (or Bye), the elder sister of both her father and TR who had married an admiral and become Mrs. Sheffield Cowles. And, of course, the occasional visits to Hyde Park and Campobello (in spite of the separate cottage) continued under the overall control of Sara Roosevelt. (The Franklin Roosevelts' Manhattan house was let to Thomas W. Lamont, the most important of J. P. Morgan's associates, who was to be the quintessential public-spirited, internationally oriented American banker of the interwar years.) Eleanor at first lived almost as circumscribed a life in Washington as she had done in New York. Her main nonnursery activity in the eighteen months before August 1914 was paying formal calls and leaving visiting cards. But when war came (even if only in Europe to begin with) it gave her a new purpose and to some extent a new independence. She became a tremendous organizer of and active provider of comforts for the troops. Hardly a naval or military train could pass through

Union Station without Eleanor being there with a bevy of assistants to hand out hot drinks, cigarettes, buns, and knitted socks. This and associated activities assuaged her need for commitment if not for intellectual stimulation.

She was away for long summers. In 1916, the year of the first great polio epidemic, when there were 2,448 deaths (mostly of children) in New York City, she was in Campobello or Hyde Park for the best part of three months. This was partly because FDR, ironically in view of the future, regarding polio as essentially a children's disease and showing a great concern for his five, dissuaded her from bringing them to any likely center of infection, and eventually sent (with doubtful propriety) a navy vessel to bring them from Maine and up the Hudson to Hyde Park without touching land in the cesspit of the city. The voyage was reluctantly undertaken under the command of William Leahy; a quarter of a century later, Roosevelt was to send him as ambassador to Vichy France.

It was probably in this summer that Roosevelt's infatuation with Lucy Mercer, his wife's part-time social secretary, became serious. Miss Mercer was far from being a bimbo. She was only twenty-two, but a young lady of good family and delicate charm if not, as her employment implied, of secure wealth. She was a quintessential Jane Austen heroine, cast up a hundred years late on the shores of the District of Columbia rather than of those of Dorset or Devon. Some, perhaps most notably the worldly Alice Longworth, thought it amazing that Franklin had not strayed earlier. However, stray he did, not casually but romantically, and in an underlying sense not temporarily but to the very end of his life. Eleanor's favorite poem, with its line "unless you can die when the dream is past," came to have a terrible validity, but not for her.

Despite his fine appearance of vaulting virility, Franklin's health as a young man was not very good. In this he was no different from many statesmen of exceptional energy and achievement. Gladstone, whose physical and mental achievements throughout his life of eighty-nine years were sufficient to make most people feel tired, was constantly taking to his bed. FDR was not far off emulating him. In the summer of 1911, he was dragged down by sinus trouble in Albany and Eleanor had to return from Campobello to nurse him. In the autumn of 1912, he was incapacitated for almost the whole of the campaign by typhoid fever (which Eleanor also caught) and his new henchman, Louis Howe, a wizened monkey of a journalist, had to fight it on his behalf. In the summer of 1917, he developed a throat infection severe enough to send him to the hospital and to see Eleanor again recalled from Campobello. In September 1918, he returned from his trip to the European theater with double pneumonia. He had to be driven by ambulance from the ship to his mother's New York house and carried indoors by four navy enlisted men. In early 1919, uncomfortably soon after his pneumonia, he caught the virulent influenza that was sweeping Europe and America. So, even before his great affliction of 1921, he was no stranger to illness. His air of lissome health was more a matter of appearance than of reality.

In the course of handling FDR's correspondence during his bout of pneumonia, Eleanor came across some of the letters from Lucy Mercer, and was left in no doubt about the nature of the relationship, although she had probably had her suspicions for a year or so before. This discovery, which sophisticates like Alice Longworth thought she should certainly have been expecting in view of the contrasting attitudes to relaxation and pleasure between herself and her husband, and also thought she should have taken in her stride, was a tremendous blow to Eleanor. It did not destroy the marriage, although divorce was discussed and then rejected, but it changed its nature. The relationship had never been physically passionate, although on Eleanor's side it had been deeply romantic, one of the "Idylls of the King" in Tennysonian style. Thereafter it became a powerful political partnership, but almost a limited-liability one. The legend of Guinevere and Sir Lancelot was replaced by that of Sidney and Beatrice Webb, the British husband-and-wife social reformers of the early twentieth century, except that Franklin had more of the spirit of Beatrice and Eleanor more the devotion to duty of Sidney.

Eleanor was considerably assisted in her acceptance of the new status and the transition to a more political role by two factors. First, in the decision not to go for a divorce, with much stress put upon the interests of the five children, Franklin may also have been affected by Miss Mercer's Roman Catholic attitude to remarriage as well as by the damage that divorce would have done to his political prospects. Eleanor was mollified by promises that she, possibly unwisely, extracted from Franklin that he would totally rupture his relations with Lucy Mercer. Broadly he stuck to this promise for twenty years or so, although he is said to have arranged for her to attend his first inaugural as president — a harmless enough twitch upon the thread, it may be thought — but not to the very end. He was assisted in this long abstinence by Lucy's marriage, seventeen months after Eleanor's discovery of the letters, to Mr. Winthrop Rutherfurd, a rich, respectable, and middle-aged gentleman, who died in early 1944.

The second factor was the already mentioned Louis Howe. He was a man fascinated by the political process and dedicated to vicarious political success. Believing that his own lack of physical charisma precluded him from achieving it for himself, he decided to hitch his wagon to a star, and the star he chose, as early as 1911, was Franklin Roosevelt. And he remained hitched until his death in 1936. He was a great asset, for he had not only dedication and total loyalty, but also an exceptionally shrewd political sense. He was not an ideologue. He wanted the optimum success for his chosen principal, and he was more interested in moves that would bring this about than in any particular views. He was one of two "body servants" of exceptional quality and, up to a point, independent judgment whom FDR was lucky to attract to his service. The second was Harry Hopkins, who was of even higher quality than Howe.

At first the Roosevelt women — Sara and Eleanor were in rare agreement — did not like Howe. They both thought him a common and cocky little journalist; "that dirty little man," Sara called him, and Eleanor began by agreeing. Sara probably never much shifted her view, although Howe's value to Franklin forced her somewhat to dissimulate; she went as far as having the Howe family (he had a daughter at Vassar, just down the river) several times to stay at Hyde Park. Eleanor, on the other hand, changed dramatically, in her heart as well as in her behavior. This was due partly to her increasingly broad outlook and partly to Howe's skillful cultivation of her. He asked for her opinion on political matters, and by so doing increased her confidence to an extent that made her advice worthwhile as well as tactically wise to seek. By 1920–21 they were firm friends and allies.

Over these couple of years, the two formative setbacks of Franklin Roosevelt's life occurred. For the 1920 presidential election, he was nominated with extraordinary ease as Democratic candidate for the vice presidency. The ease may have stemmed from the lack of attraction of the prize. In retrospect at least, the Democrats were on a branch line to nowhere. With the Democratic tide having run its course, with Wilson incapacitated and his policies increasingly unpopular, their chances of winning were negligible. Governor James M. Cox of Ohio headed the ticket, and Roosevelt's appeal as running mate was his name and his combination of youth and wartime experience in Washington. The attraction for him, even though he was also adding himself to the list of some of the least remembered men in American politics — defeated vice presidential candidates — was that he was once again following in the footsteps of Theodore Roosevelt, and doing so even younger again: at thirty-eight, where TR had been forty-two. The difference was that TR was part of a winning ticket, whereas FDR lost, and then had to wait another twelve years to achieve the greater accolade.

Cox and Roosevelt fought a thoroughly

respectable campaign, standing firm for Wilson's commitment to American participation in the League of Nations. FDR was personally well received in his tours across the continent and made useful party friends for the future. He committed only one gaffe, but it was in character with his overconfident and overgrown puppy attitude to politics at the time. In Butte, Montana, he sought to counter the argument that Britain, with its dominions, would have six votes in the League Assembly to one for the United States by saying that the latter would have a bevy of Central American client states, and so clear was this subordinate relationship that in the case of Haiti he had even written the constitution himself.

The November result was devastating. The popular vote, in the first election with female suffrage, was 16 million for the "front porch" (that is, nonactive) campaign of Warren G. Harding, as cardboard a figure as ever occupied the presidency, against 9 million for the Cox-Roosevelt ticket. This was proportionately a greater preponderance than the 27 million to 16 million that Roosevelt was to score in his revenge of 1936, although because the South was still relatively solid for the Democrats in 1920, that year's election did not produce nearly such a clean sweep of the electoral college.

Once again Roosevelt's "Teflon" quality showed itself. Being a junior partner in this debacle did his reputation remarkably little harm. He withdrew from Washington to New York, set himself up in an undemanding job as vice president of a bonding company, and awaited his political future with equanimity. Then, in the first August after his vice presidential campaign, he was stricken at Campobello by poliomyelitis, which five years before he had treated with such apprehension, although essentially as a children's disease. The story of how on a sailing expedition the family went ashore to fight a forest fire and how FDR, after jogging back toward the house, first had a very cold swim in the Bay of Fundy and then sat in his wet bathing suit skimming the mail that had just arrived is too well known to need detailed repetition. The next morning he was partially paralyzed and returned to bed. He never again walked unaided.

Roosevelt's period of semirecovery, combined with his acceptance of a new debility, reducing but not crushing, can be regarded as lasting thirty-five months, until the Democratic convention in New York City in July 1924, when he reimprinted his personality upon national politics with his "Happy Warrior" speech nominating Governor Al Smith as presidential candidate. It did not get Smith the nomination, although it helped him fight on through a hundred ballots before both Smith and his main rival, William McAdoo, Wilson's son-in-law and a former secretary of the treasury, withdrew in favor of a colorless compromise (John W. Davis), who proceeded to poll little less than 30 percent of the vote and to be slaughtered by the monosyllabic Calvin Coolidge.

FDR's struggle to get back to any active role was not only long but also demoralizing. At first, the seriousness of his illness was underestimated. An esteemed physician was summoned to Campobello from Philadelphia and proceeded to make a spectacular misdiagnosis. He ruled out infantile paralysis (polio) and thought the problem was a blood clot that would certainly clear itself up. Then a still more esteemed New York doctor came from Newport, Rhode Island, where he was vacationing, and got it right, accompanied by a somber but not hopeless prognosis. In September, Roosevelt was removed by boat to New York and went into Presbyterian Hospital, where he remained until October 28. This was a depressing period, for it became clear that he was not going to recover quickly, if at all, and he also suffered great continuing pain.

Sara Roosevelt had returned from a European trip at the end of August, and there then began a great clash of wills between her and the newly formed alliance of Eleanor and Louis Howe. Sara wanted Franklin to react to his illness by emulating her husband and his father, who had not even required the excuse of paralyzed limbs to withdraw from the vulgar arena to the life of an invalid country gentleman. Eleanor and Howe were determined that he should spring back to full political activity. Their motives were somewhat different but not in conflict. Eleanor, even though early Washington may have been something of a liberation for her, was miserable there in 1919–20, after the Lucy Mercer contretemps. She may have exorcised Miss Mercer, but she must increasingly have felt a sense of there being a specter at the feast while Franklin, maybe as a reaction against being deprived of Lucy, sought fresh gaiety with increasing determination. A combination of the 1920 campaign (during which there developed her alliance with Howe) and the move back to New

York somewhat freed Eleanor from that incubus.

Louis Howe's motives were in a sense less complicated. He still had total faith in his crippled master, and believed that even after the massive setback of 1921 he could be propelled to the political heights. And this belief was vindicated to an extent beyond even Howe's wildest dreams. The man who left the hospital at the end of October with a bleak prognosis and the ability to do little more with his legs than wiggle his toes was to become the longest serving of all presidents and the dominant American political personality of the twentieth century. The credit for this spectacular recovery not of physical vigor (for that was terribly slow and partial) but of authority and public persona lies in the buoyant willpower of Franklin D. Roosevelt himself. Eleanor and Howe were important auxiliaries, but they could never have done it without the spirit of the principal.

No doubt there were private dark nights of the soul; Eleanor, who wrote of 1921–22 as "the most trying winter" of her life, probably had to put up with heavy bouts of gloom and bad temper. There was little enough room for optimism. In his first month at home after the hospital, it seemed as though Franklin's problems were not merely orthopedic. He again ran high temperatures, and his vision was thought to be threatened. And then, nearly a year later, when he paid a first hesitant visit to the financial district office of the Fidelity and Deposit bonding company (his job had been kept open), he fell while making his way on crutches across the large and slippery floor of the lobby. It was a humiliation as well as a jolt, but he is said to have summoned up a burst of apparently spontaneous laughter, with which he relaxed the tension on the faces of those who clustered around him. Such public gaiety, fortunately not often having to be delivered from a marble floor, became a feature of his postpolio public style. His doctors commented on his smiling good manners. It was not that Roosevelt accepted his new disability with martyred resignation. He was constantly seeking new methods to overcome it, and constantly believing, against the likelihood, that he would be restored. Nor did he ever remotely seek public sympathy for his weakness. He was determined to hide it as far as was humanly possible (that is one reason why his laughter at that 1922 fall was so remarkable) and substantially succeeded with the

American public. Even during his presidency very few had any idea how much time he spent in a wheelchair.

There has long been argument as to what extent Roosevelt's paralysis changed and deepened his character, making him a more mature and serious figure, better suited to the presidency. "Change of character" may be putting it too high, but clearly the illness strengthened his tendency to dissimulate, to charm people while revealing as little about himself as possible. He increasingly kept his views secret behind a surface of optimistic geniality. It was not entirely a coincidence that he signaled his return to public life in 1924 by what became famous as his "Happy Warrior" speech, and that eight years later the campaign song for his first presidential election was "Happy Days Are Here Again."

Alfred E. Smith, whom the speech put into nomination, was about as different from Roosevelt as it is possible to imagine — that was a large part of the reason why Roosevelt had been asked to perform the nominating role. In the 1920s, they were at first wary allies, and then in the 1930s, when Roosevelt had clearly emerged as top dog, increasingly separated enemies. Smith was born eight years before Roosevelt. He was a poor boy from the heart of the Bowery, on Manhattan's Lower East Side. One of his most dramatic childhood memories was watching the building of the Brooklyn Bridge. In spite of his family name he was far from being of Anglo-Saxon stock, let alone old Dutch. He was mainly Irish on his mother's side. The only point at which his maternal grandfather's life touched that of the Roosevelts was that he worked for many years as a tailor's assistant for Brooks Brothers, from which esteemed establishment FDR was many years later to get a lot of his clothes. On his father's side, Smith was mostly Italian, although he also had a German grandmother. He was a quintessential product of the melting pot of late-nineteenth-century New York City.

In New York State, he was a charismatic figure with a good record as a progressive Albany politician extending back to 1904. By 1924 he had already served two separated terms as governor. He had long had the devoted loyalty of Frances Perkins, later to be one of FDR's most progressive and successful Cabinet officers. And Eleanor Roosevelt worked enthusiastically for him in his fourth gubernatorial contest later in that same year of 1924. But Smith was a divisive figure across the nation. He had no appeal to rural America. He was a Roman Catholic, virulently wet in the Prohibition argument, and in every detail dressed to express the outlook of a city slicker. His campaign song, "The Sidewalks of New York," was distinctly low on appeal west of the Alleghenies. As a result the Democratic convention was deeply divided, which was why the voting went to 103 ballots. Nevertheless, there was every reason why Roosevelt, even apart from his great need to reproject himself, should have been content to nominate Smith.

About this nominating speech there were two ambiguities. The first ambiguity was whether Roosevelt wrote it himself or whether Smith's campaign manager, Judge Joseph M. Proskauer, did most of it for him. Undoubtedly it was Proskauer who provided the key Wordsworth lines of "This is the happy Warrior; this is he/That every man in arms should wish to be," which FDR at first resisted on the grounds that they were too high-flown. The second ambiguity was how long the speech lasted. One account says seventeen minutes, another thirty-four. They are reconcilable, however, according to whether or not the strenuous demonstration that occurred when he first mentioned Smith's name is counted. The first certainty is that it cost FDR a tremendous effort — on crutches and on the arm of his sixteen-year-old eldest son — to get to the podium. And the second certainty is that once he got there he seized the audience and scored a tremendous success. Even the often critical Walter Lippmann wrote of it (admittedly to Roosevelt himself) as "perfect in temper and manner and most eloquent in its effect," while Smith himself said that Roosevelt was "the most impressive figure in the Convention."

FDR did not get the nomination for Smith — after his speech he might have found it easier to get it for himself — but he saved Smith from a crushing defeat and paved the way for Smith to secure the nomination in 1928 after another two terms of successful governorship. Roosevelt thereby created the vacancy that led to his own election as governor of New York. Even more strikingly, FDR had reemerged on the national political scene, and had done so with tremendous éclat.

3

From Albany to the White House

The years from 1924 to 1928 were a semi-lacuna in Roosevelt's life. Less happened than in almost any other four years, and thus in retrospect the time seems to have gone by remarkably quickly, although maybe the years themselves seemed to have been dragging. Put briefly, there were four main aspects to his life. He gave first place to an increasingly utopian attempt to recover full use of his legs. This involved spending much of the winters (and some other seasons, too) at a dilapidated resort in western Georgia called Warm Springs, which he discovered in 1924. Warm Springs, about eighty miles south of Atlanta and fairly close to the Alabama state line, quickly replaced the long houseboat cruises in the semitropical Florida waters that had been his previous habit.

At the same time, Roosevelt kept up a sporadic New York business life. His bonding firm, Fidelity and Deposit, did rather well, mainly because of FDR's exploitation of his contacts from public life, which were important to that specialized insurance business. He also indulged during that get-rich-quick decade in a number of highly speculative separate enterprises, some of them involving the setting up of companies to develop very doubtful new products. Most of these failed, probably canceling out any profits he made from Fidelity and Deposit, and exemplifying the sound general principle that there is an almost inverse relationship — save for John Maynard Keynes — between those who improve the performance of national economies and those who look after their own finances well.

The third development of these years was that Eleanor created for herself an increasingly independent life, devoted in a sense to Franklin's interests in that she worked indefatigably for the Democratic party in New York State and also kept alive his political contacts, reporting their views and inviting the most favored to go and see him at Warm Springs. She built up an intense network of female friends, of which the camaraderie is well illustrated by a contemporary photograph. Her second surviving son, Elliott, named after her adored but feckless father and having at

least some of his unsatisfactory characteristics and therefore not a totally reliable
witness, although often close to his
mother, described this group by saying
that Eleanor "had a sort of compulsion to
associate with fellow sufferers in frustration, women like herself who had found it
impossible to get along with the opposite
sex." However, her closest relationship of
this sort, with Lorena Hickok, a journalist
who began by interviewing Eleanor during
the 1932 presidential campaign and then
became an inseparable companion, did not
start until that later date.

Sara Roosevelt did not much like this nest
of women, but Franklin gave no sign of dis-
approval, and indeed encouraged the
building of Val-Kill Cottage, on his mother's
Hyde Park estate, although satisfactorily separated from the big house by being two
miles away on the landward side of the old
post road to Albany. There, in ungrandiose
but comfortable circumstances, Eleanor held
her own female court. One of the courtiers,
Nancy Cook, an efficient lady in mannish
suits and with cropped curly hair, but with a
much better aesthetic eye than Eleanor, set
up a successful cottage industry, making
good reproductions of Early American fur-
niture. In a quiet way it prospered more

than Franklin's bolder but more ill-judged ventures.

Meanwhile the Roosevelt children were growing up, and not wholly satisfactorily. In 1927 Anna was twenty-one, James twenty, Elliott seventeen, Franklin thirteen, and John eleven. Their education was more conventional than successful. Endicott Peabody had to cope with the four boys at Groton, despite Elliott's strong preference for going to the local high school at Hyde Park. Harvard received three (Elliott again being the refusenik, and on this occasion a more effective one), but did not achieve much academically for any of the three. Anna made an unsuccessful marriage to a New York stockbroker at the age of twenty, and divorced him six years later. James, at twenty-one, got himself engaged to Betsey Cushing, one of the three daughters of a Boston surgeon, who were notable equally for their beauty and for their marriages. Eleanor, when she first met Betsey, described her as "a nice child," a mildly patronizing description of her first daughter-in-law, who in Eleanor's many absences was to be a cosseting hostess for FDR in the White House, and then, her marriage to James having proved as impermanent as most of the Roosevelt unions of that generation, became Mrs. John Hay Whitney and a notable ambassadorial hostess in London in the 1950s. But Eleanor was perhaps more generous than Sara Roosevelt, who on her first encounter with Miss Cushing is reported to have said: "I understand your father is a surgeon — surgeons always remind me of my butcher," thereby showing that American snobbery could at least hold a candle to the allegedly much more extreme English version.

Franklin, partly by nature, partly by geography, remained aloof from most of the adolescent and postadolescent problems of his children. It could be said that the main function of the boys was to provide an arm on which he could lean for his dramatic advances to oratorical podiums. James did it for the 1924 Democratic convention, Elliott for the 1928 one, and Franklin Junior and John on several notable later occasions. Anna, who in 1934 married John Boettiger, a Chicago journalist, was a good alternate to Betsey in providing White House company for FDR during the war years.

Apart from keeping his oar in politics, about which Howe and Eleanor were more determined than he was, Franklin's main interest in these late 1920s years was in the Warm Springs spa. In 1926 he bought the whole establishment — the spring, the somewhat primitive swimming pool to which it gave a natural temperature of eighty-nine degrees Fahrenheit, the run-down hotel, and a surrounding thousand acres with a few cottages — for $200,000. This was a substantial sum of money at the time. It was most of the money he had inherited from his father, although there was always his rich mother in reserve. She could be depended upon for necessary supplements, even if only at the price of underlining his dependence. It was therefore highly desirable that he make Warm Springs pay, and this he broadly succeeded in doing. He installed an orthopedic surgeon and a team of physiotherapists, built a second, covered pool, spruced up the hotel and its surrounding buildings, increased their capacity to sixty-one patients, and, most important, built a cottage for himself, which became, with Hyde Park, one of his two favorite retreats. From 1927 until he died there in April 1945, it was a crucial part of his life.

This increased his separation, physical and emotional, from Eleanor. Her orderly temperament, which could not see a slovenly scene without wishing to improve it, made her dislike the Deep South with its rural squalor and, in those days, rigid racial segregation. He was still more a product of the ordered landscape and relative prosperity of the Hudson Valley than she was, but his more easygoing nature made him accept with curiosity rather than distaste the disordered poverty of that part of the South. There was also a personal factor at work. Just as Eleanor regarded Hyde Park as Sara Roosevelt's domain and never felt at home there until she built Val-Kill Cottage, so she regarded Warm Springs as being the domain of Missy LeHand, who had been Roosevelt's principal personal secretary since January 1921, and was to remain so until a stroke in 1941. Missy was pretty, quite stylish, and utterly devoted to Roosevelt. She was almost invariably at Warm Springs when FDR was, habitually managed the house there, and did so in a way that he found less austere and more relaxing than was Eleanor's habit. He was totally at ease in her company and undoubtedly very fond of her, although (admittedly with a lot of other things on his mind at that time) he rather forgot about her in the three years between her stroke and her death in 1944. Eleanor, who felt half warm toward Missy and half jealous of her, apparently had to press him to make at least Christmas telephone calls to her during this period. The jealous half was at least sufficient to make Eleanor avoid Warm Springs.

FDR had renominated Smith for governor at the 1926 New York State Democratic convention, and was the natural choice to repeat his 1924 role at the Houston national convention in the summer of 1928. He went without Eleanor and on this occasion got to the podium without crutches, although heavily supported by Elliott, who had become a Texas resident. More demanding than this physical feat, however, was the challenge of preventing this repeat performance from flopping after his 1924 triumph. This challenge he impressively surmounted. It was part of Roosevelt's quality that he hardly ever failed to summon up the combination of personality, adrenaline, and words required for a major occasion. The *New York Times* gave the speech a full accolade, saying it fully matched his "Happy Warrior" speech.

This time Smith secured the nomination. Indeed, he got it sufficiently easily that Roosevelt's speech cannot be regarded as a crucial factor. The Democratic nomination in 1928 was, however, almost as much of a poisoned chalice as that of 1924 would have been. A combination of prosperity in urban areas (there was no faltering for another year) and Smith's weakness in rural appeal guaranteed the election of Herbert Hoover. Smith polled nearly twice as well as Davis had done in 1924, but the Republican vote also went up, and the tally was the decisive one of 21.5 million to 15 million. Smith even failed to carry the state of which he had been governor for four terms.

As he began his national campaign, Smith greatly wanted Roosevelt to take his place as Democratic candidate for the New York governorship. He thought that FDR would be a strong vote-getter upstate and that the votes so pulled for him for governor would also be cast for Smith for president. He also thought that Roosevelt would be a weak governor, so that if Smith did not himself get to Washington he could continue to pull the strings in Albany. Roosevelt was indeed a good vote attracter, but all Smith's other assumptions were false, and out of his misapprehensions there sprang the rupture between these two men. On this thesis Smith hatched a plot by which Roosevelt would head the ticket while Herbert Lehman, later a notably liberal senator from New York, would run for lieutenant governor and be prepared, when Roosevelt continued to spend long months immersing his legs at Warm Springs, to do most of the work both of the campaign and then at Albany, the latter under the beneficent direction of Smith.

This, more tactfully put, was the proposition that Smith endeavored to sell to Roosevelt by telephone to Warm Springs at the end of September. At first Roosevelt was resistant, mainly because Louis Howe was advising him that 1928 was going to be another year of all-around Democratic defeat. But he eventually agreed that he would accept a draft and was nominated by acclamation, on the proposition of the extremely dodgy Mayor Jimmy Walker of New York, on October 2. Robert Moses, who had been Smith's secretary of state in the Albany administration and was later to create much of the visible sinew of modern New York City, from the Triborough Bridge to the East River Drive (now the Franklin D. Roosevelt Drive), summed up the attitude of the Smith establishment by muttering to Governor Smith's daughter during the acclaim, "He'll make a good candidate but a lousy governor."

There then followed the collapse of Smith's assumptions. First, Roosevelt fought a vigorous campaign. He did not just give "a couple of raddio speeches," as Smith with his eccentric pronunciation of the word for that new medium had suggested. FDR was sufficiently restored to be able to move around the state with considerable vigor and to get, with difficulty, from a train or car to a platform in a local hall. He was already a formidable campaigner, with a confidence-giving beam from under a battered felt hat, even if from a sedentary position, having an electrifying effect. Smith contributed a rather good reply to those who said that Roosevelt's physical condition was not up to the job: "A governor does not have to be an acrobat. We do not elect him for his ability to do a double back-flip or a handspring." His opponent was an able Republican ex–attorney general, Albert Ottinger, who some thought would pull in the New York City vote by virtue of his Jewishness. There was even a suggestion that a politically split ticket of "Al and Al" would triumph. This could hardly have been more wrong. Smith lost his own state by more than 100,000, and Roosevelt won by the narrow margin of 25,000 in a total poll of 4.2 million.

Louis Howe, opposed though he had

been to FDR's entry into the contest, recognized the significance of the result much more clearly than did Smith. Howe, although he got someone else to say it first, immediately subscribed to the view that "we've got the next president." Smith still thought he could treat Roosevelt as his surrogate, and was surprised and affronted when Roosevelt declined to keep on, as part of his official Albany family, either Robert Moses or the formidable Belle Moskowitz, Smith's long-standing and powerful executive secretary. This started the cutting free that led eight years later to Smith leading the Liberty League campaign against Roosevelt on the eve of his second term. When Smith came to Washington to deliver his 1936 anti–New Deal philippic, Eleanor Roosevelt asked him to stay in the White House on the grounds that he was an old friend, although one who had moved far to the right of FDR, while she had moved somewhat to the left. Such are the paradoxes of American politics and, fortunately, also those of a few other countries. Smith had the good sense to decline the invitation, and with that more or less disappeared from the Roosevelt story.

How good a governor was Roosevelt? He

was always a temporary lodger in the Executive Mansion at Albany, not because, as Smith had complacently thought, he would spend most of his time at Warm Springs or, maybe, as Smith also thought, die within a year. It was more because he was from the beginning a train in transit at Albany rather than one that had reached its destination. He was a president in waiting, from the beginning in the eyes of a few Howe-led aficionados, and more generally after his 1930 reelection, which saw him increase his margin of victory from the 25,000 of 1928 to 725,000. His priorities in the prominent, powerful, yet geographically confined role of governor (difficult to understand for an Englishman habituated to the weak rotating mayors of provincial cities and great control from the center) had been to concentrate upon public electric power and support for agriculture. This seemed to have worked, although no doubt disenchantment with Republican orthodoxy, which set in with the end of the boom years, had an even greater effect.

An important figure who came into the picture at this stage was James A. Farley. Farley, without a background of much interest, became an essential man of political business for Roosevelt. He was a professional politician, lacking — on the surface, at any rate — much ideology or hinterland outside politics. In his old age, when I met him, he had a certain style. Somewhat surprisingly, he was a guest in the official box at a (relatively) grand cricket match in London. He wore a jaunty straw boater and was introduced to Alec Douglas Home and to me. He addressed us both with courtesy but with obvious incomprehension of the identity of either of us (Home was a former prime minister), then bade us good-bye with a lift of his hat and a vaguely patronizing salutation: "It has been a privilege to meet you two gentlemen."

Farley's main role in the runup to the 1932 Democratic National Convention was to go across the continent, nominally in his capacity as a popular member of the Benevolent and Protective Order of Elks to attend their convention in Seattle. The destination was well chosen. It enabled him to cover eighteen states in nineteen days and to perform a brilliant soft-sell mission for Roosevelt. He did his job with affability rather than hardness. His line was to say that there were three possible candidates of quality: Smith, who was in fact already dead in the water; Owen D. Young, who had earlier produced a plan to stabilize the German mark when it was falling catastrophically from hour to hour but whose current job was head of the General Electric Company at a time when American faith in captains of industry was tumbling nearly as fast as the reichsmark had done; and Roosevelt. Perhaps not surprisingly, Farley found a groundswell of support for his chosen third candidate. He then became Roosevelt's floor manager at the Chicago convention of the following summer, and was rewarded when the 1933 administration was put together by the patronage-dispensing office of postmaster general. This gave him control not only over who should be postmasters (and postmistresses) around the Union, but over a wider range of federal appointments as well. By the standards of the time, he exercised these powers with relative propriety, although never forgetting the interests of the Democratic party and of his role within it. Unlike Smith, he remained faithful to Roosevelt for his second presidential contest in 1936, but by 1940 he had got ideas above his station, conceived presidential ambitions for himself, and opposed FDR running for a third term. It was as though Fouché, the prefect of police, had thought that he might displace the emperor Napoleon. Thereafter Farley was in outer darkness, even though he became chairman of the Coca-Cola Export Corporation. It was nonetheless not without a certain significance that Roosevelt had by this time lost not only Smith, who had propelled him into the governorship, but also Farley, who had done much to make him president.

In the contest for the 1932 Democratic nomination, Roosevelt was always the front-runner but never the certain winner — often a vulnerable position. His main rivals were the unelectable but nearly indestructible Al Smith, backed by the big-money element in the Democratic party and commanding a majority of the New York delegation, and John Nance Garner, the Texan Speaker of the House of Representatives. Roosevelt's lead was enormous but not quite sufficient for him to be nominated on the first ballot, thanks to the "two-thirds rule." This had long stultified Democratic conventions, often forcing them to adopt weak compromise candidates — which, indeed, was part of the reason why, of the fourteen presidents between the Civil War and 1932, only two had been Democrats. But the South regarded the rule as a protection of its interests against the adoption of dangerous northern liberals, and the Roosevelt forces had burnt their fingers by trying unsuccessfully to get it changed at the beginning of this Chicago convention.

On the first vote, which was taken between four and seven in the morning of July 1, thereby showing that a liking for taking momentous decisions at inappropriate hours is no monopoly of the British House of Commons, Roosevelt had 666½ votes of the 769 he required, with 203¾ for Smith and 90¼ for Garner (precision counting was a feature of conventions of those days). The position looked impregnable, but this was by no means the case, particularly when another two ballots before the adjournment at nine a.m. yielded only a marginal Roosevelt gain. The prospect of a compromise candidate was beginning to loom. The likely beneficiary was Newton D. Baker, who had been Wilson's secretary of war and remained a firm Wilsonian internationalist — more so than Roosevelt, who, to the dismay of his wife and some others, had reneged on his commitment to American membership in the League of Nations in a speech on February 2.

The threat of Baker was skillfully played by Joseph P. Kennedy, beginning to emerge on the national scene as a presidential broker nearly three decades before he became a presidential father. Kennedy used it to persuade William Randolph Hearst, the great newspaper tycoon who falsely believed himself to be a great politician as well, to tell Garner, of whom he had been a principal backer, that the time had come to release his Texas votes to Roosevelt. The other key fixer was William McAdoo, who had originally been pro-Smith (paradoxically, in view of their 1924 rivalry), but who could tell a hawk from a handsaw and had decided he did not want another stultified convention. "California came here to nominate a president of the United States," he said in the key speech of the nominating process. "She did not come here to deadlock this convention." But he had privately laid down his own terms: Garner for vice president, control over California patronage, and a right of veto over the appointments to head the State Department and the Treasury. These two shifts put Roosevelt well over the required quota. He had 942 votes; only a recalcitrant 202½, including a majority of the New York State delegation and four other eastern states, all part of the territory in which Roosevelt was most at home, remained as a sullen pro-Smith redoubt.

Roosevelt had therefore been decisively but not gloriously nominated. Deals had been necessary on the way. These assisted but did not create the ambiguity of the platform upon which he fought. That ambiguity was more in his mind, and was undiminished by the variety of advisers and speechwriters whom he had assembled. His tactical advisers were Howe, who had the advantage of the longest relationship; Farley, who had that of his successful Elk-stalking across the continent; and Edward J. Flynn, a Democratic chieftain of the Bronx, whom a combination of the East River and an intellectual fastidiousness made anti-Tammany. Roosevelt made him his secretary of state at Albany in place of Smith's man Moses. Flynn was to remain faithful to Roosevelt well after Howe had died and Farley had defected. Sam Rosenman was an intellectual lawyer who was counsel to the governor and interpreted his public service duties flexibly enough to be able to write most of Roosevelt's acceptance speech for Chicago. But he was about to accept an appointment to the New York Supreme Court, and was therefore hobbled. In the meantime, however, he had introduced Roosevelt to Raymond Moley, a law professor at Columbia, who was the first member of the so-called brain trust. What these members had in common was that they all came from Columbia University, mainly because the Roosevelt machine was not at that stage particularly well heeled, and preferred not to have to pay the train fares from Yale, much less from Harvard. But they did not have much else in common. Moley was a William Jennings Bryan man, which made him both isolationist and rather right wing on economic policy in the context of 1932. He overplayed his hand at the World Economic Conference in the summer of 1933, behaving as though he were a law unto himself until he was pulled back by Cordell Hull, the old Tennessee politician who had become FDR's new secretary of state.

Moley introduced another Columbia professor, Rexford G. Tugwell, an agricultural economist, into the team. Tugwell had a flexibility of doctrine and sharpness of mind and conversation that endeared him to Roosevelt. With Adolf A. Berle, a Harvard man (college and law school), now a brilliant member of the Columbia Law School faculty, they constituted the early core of the brain trust. It was not a very coordinated core; even had it been, its members would have been somewhat at odds with the older nonacademic advisers.

When the news of his nomination came through to Albany, Roosevelt decided to fly at once to Chicago to accept the nomination. This was a calculated break with the tradition — which, although not invariably applied, was that the candidate sat modestly on his "front porch" until a delegation from the convention slowly arrived, traveling as it were by "horse and buggy" (to use a phrase that Roosevelt himself was to make famous three years later), and graciously offered him the nomination. The flight to Chicago was also a skillful move, designed to show both that FDR was to be a president for a new era and that he was in no way a prisoner of his physical infirmity.

It was not, however, an easy move to carry out. Civilian flying, even five years after Lindbergh's Atlantic adventure, was still in its infancy. Roosevelt's small flying party comprised Eleanor, two sons, Sam Rosenman, two secretaries (Missy LeHand and her junior Grace Tully), and two state troopers as bodyguards. (One of the bodyguards, Earl Miller, was to become almost as much a part of the domestic court, particularly to Eleanor, as the legendary gruff Highlander John Brown was of Queen

Victoria's.) The trip took them nine hours, including a refueling stop in Buffalo and much battling against headwinds. It was perhaps no accident that Roosevelt never flew again until he went to the Casablanca Conference eleven years later.

Nor did the battling cease when they got on the ground. Louis Howe, who with Farley had been in the front line of the smoke-filled rooms, exploded when he saw the Rosenman-drafted speech Roosevelt proposed to deliver that evening. In the event, a mild compromise was achieved. Roosevelt surmounted both the dispute and the somewhat inchoate nature of his platform by the confidence of his delivery and the magnetism of his personality; "I pledge you, I pledge myself, to a new deal for the American people" was the phrase from the speech that stuck.

Roosevelt's 1932 campaign had the major advantage that it was from the beginning fairly clearly a winning ticket. That, even before the result, has considerable advantages. It means that small crevices are not dangerous. A faltering candidate falls into them. A winning one skims over them. Hoover made an even more decisive contribution to losing the election than Roosevelt did to winning it. The combination of a downward-spiraling economy and the rigid negativeness of Hoover's approach was deadly. By the time of the election, production, employment, and prices in the nonfarm sectors of the economy had been falling steadily for two years, joining a stock market that had been falling for almost three and a farming economy that had been in recession for at least six. Four months later, the country's banking system fell apart. Hoover, looking back to previous depressions with the eyes of a classical economist and a fairly strict constitutionalist, saw nothing for it but retrenchment and patience, tempered by some unorthodox loans to business. By late 1932, unemployment had extended to perhaps a quarter of the labor force, an unprecedented outcome for which there seemed no ready answers in Hoover's philosophy.

His stance was epitomized by his insensitive dealing with the "bonus army." About eight thousand unemployed veterans arrived in Washington demanding payment of a delayed bonus, which, as a result of a curiously convoluted act of Congress of 1925, they were to be paid in 1945. Not unnaturally in their circumstances, they wanted it then rather than in the remote future. Hoover ordered the veterans to evacuate their camp and sent troops down Pennsylvania Avenue to attack them with sabers and tear gas. Two men were killed and fire swept through the camp.

Roosevelt condemned this gross overreaction, although, when he came in, he did not give the veterans their bonus. Indeed, his budgetary stance during the campaign was at least as austere as Hoover's. At Pittsburgh on October 19, he promised to cut the cost of government operations by 25 percent. On other occasions, however, particularly when Tugwell was speechwriting, he implied planned activity to get the economy moving again. How he imagined he was going to do that while slashing federal expenditure is not remotely clear. But at least his policy muddles were clothed in a sense of sympathy and activism, whereas Hoover's outlook, perhaps more bleakly clear, was adorned by nothing more appealing than hard-line negativism. The campaign was a triumph of style over substance, although once in office Roosevelt's actions, while still strong on style, had a good deal of substance about them.

This contrast in styles gave a special interest to the treatment of the wretched bonus-seekers. In July 1932, as we have seen, Hoover sent the military to clear them out of their camp. In the perspective of the eminence this operation's commanders were to achieve in World War II, the veterans were at least given a first-class military funeral. General Douglas MacArthur was in charge of the operation, with Major Dwight Eisenhower and Captain George Patton among his supporting officers. In the summer of 1933, the veterans, maybe this time a slightly different group, were back in camp in Washington. No troops were sent to disperse them; instead, Eleanor Roosevelt came to lead them in community singing. "Hoover sent the army, Roosevelt sent his wife" (she did not need much sending) was a naturally evoked comment.

The other crevice into which his momentum saved Roosevelt from falling was that of the turpitude of Mayor Jimmy Walker. Walker was a bon vivant, liking bribes, chorus girls, gambling, and alcohol. He almost made Al Smith look like a Pilgrim Father. But he was not too incongruous in the New York of the boom years. After 1929 he looked more out of place, and in 1932 he was subject to a major investigation for civic malfeasance. This posed a problem for Roosevelt, for whom, it should be remembered, Walker had made the nominating speech for governor in 1928. Under the constitutional arrangements, at once devolved and mixing up judicial with political functions, it was up to Roosevelt as governor to decide Walker's fate. The episode came at a most inconvenient time. The high-minded across the nation would judge Roosevelt lacking in presidential timber if he condoned Walker's behavior. On the other hand, he risked alienating Tammany and the New York Democratic machine if he was severe. Farley and Rosenman warned him that he could lose the state and consequently the election on this issue.

He began a headmasterly hearing in Albany on August 11. Pinning down Walker, whom he rather liked, was not easy. Walker pursued brilliant delaying tactics. His doctor certified that he was suffering from nervous exhaustion and needed a week of rest. Then one of his brothers died and there had to be a further adjournment for the funeral. Time that Roosevelt ought to have devoted to preparing for his national campaign was being lost. Then, suddenly, on September 1, Walker resigned. With one bound, Roosevelt was free. He had the best of both worlds. That somewhat sententious weathercock

Walter Lippmann, after his enthusiasm for Roosevelt's 1924 and 1928 nominating speeches, had in January 1932 delivered himself of one of the most damaging remarks ever made about FDR: "He is a pleasant man, who, without any important qualifications for the office, would very much like to be President." But now Lippmann gave him the seal of approval: "My own judgment has been greatly modified by the manner in which he conducted the Walker hearings. . . . I shall vote cheerfully for Governor Roosevelt."

This approval was confirmed by the electorate. On November 8, Roosevelt secured a popular majority of 22,809,638 votes to 15,758,901, which translated itself into 472 electoral college votes against 59. It was not a record-breaking landslide, but it was a very strong one. Thirty-one years after Uncle Ted and eleven years after his crippling paralysis, FDR had gained the keys to the White House, although under the old rules of leisurely accession he had to wait another four months before taking up residence.

4

The Exciting Ambiguities
of the First Term

Roosevelt's early months in the White House were a mixture of dynamism and confusion. With a touch of shrewd arrogance he refused to get involved in any joint decision making with Hoover during the lame-duck period. On the occasion of his first postelection visit to the White House (November 23, 1932) Hoover tried to persuade him to endorse an international debt settlement, and thought that he had procured Roosevelt's support. He was disappointed. The president-elect's smile of apparent agreement merely meant that (as with General de Gaulle's later and famous *"Je vous ai compris"* to the French settlers in Algiers) he had taken in the measure of what was being said. Hoover was not the first, and even more certainly not the last, to make a similar misinterpretation of Roosevelt. FDR avoided confrontation so far as he could.

He did not avoid alienating the bruised and insult-sensitive Hoover, who said (privately) that he never wanted to speak to him again. However, an early January visit to Hyde Park by the outgoing secretary of state, Henry L. Stimson, produced some softening, at any rate between himself and Roosevelt (which was as well, for Stimson was to come back into office as Roosevelt's secretary of war from 1940 to 1945), and even led to another meeting with Hoover at the White House on January 20. This was as flatly unproductive as the November one, although it did not lead to the alleged total silence of the two presidents on their joint Inaugural Day drive to the Capitol; a photograph shows that they did exchange some remarks, though perhaps their content was as bleak as the weather.

After the second White House visit, Roosevelt demonstrated his detachment from Hoover's declining administration by reverting to his pre–Warm Springs habit and going on a cruise off Florida. It nearly cost him his life and annulled his presidency before it had even begun. He disembarked at Miami on February 15, and was there subject to his sole experience of one of the assassination attempts that, successful or unsuccessful, have been the lot of many American presidents. The Secret Service was not much use, thereby illustrating the truth of that dictum of protection officers all over the world that it is impossible to guarantee safety against a determined killer who is willing to lose his own life. The mayor of Chicago, Anton Cermak, provided better protection. He was on a mission of penance, having not merely failed to support Roosevelt at the Democratic convention in his own city, but having organized a gallery claque against him. He came to make his peace, but met his death. He took the bullet intended for Roosevelt. However, he took a long time to die (and Joseph Zangara, the assassin, took even longer to get to the electric chair); so Cermak's death, together with that of Roosevelt's choice as attorney general, Senator Thomas J. Walsh of Montana, who collapsed on the train back from a late-life Cuban marriage, plus the weather and the state of the economy, cast a pall over the inauguration on March 4, 1933. The day started with a Cabinet service in the church on Lafayette Square opposite the White House. The officiant was the inevitable Endicott Peabody, despite his having voted for Hoover. (Did Roosevelt know?)

It was part of Roosevelt's genius that —

much more than the rector of Groton — he cut through the gloom of a harsh March day (flags at half mast, Hoover unsmiling, and, above all, an economy in near paralysis) like a sunbeam through a lowering sky. His most memorable symbols — a cigarette (long before nicotine was regarded as poison) in a long holder at a jaunty angle and a battered old fedora hat, which proclaimed his unpompous social assurance — could not be displayed that day. On the Capitol steps he could not smoke and he had to wear, or at least convey, a silk top hat. But even without these props his greatest single attribute — his confidence-giving confidence — shone through.

His Cabinet-making, which was going on apace during the later winter months, was on balance uninspired. Among his Democratic appointments, there were also several Republicans. However, apart from his choice of Vice President Garner, who made less of an impact in that inherently unsatisfying job than Henry Wallace, Richard Nixon, Lyndon Johnson, Hubert Humphrey, George H. W. Bush, and Dick Cheney were to do, there was no reaching out to those in the party who had not supported him. There was no offer to Newton Baker or William McAdoo, still less to Al

Smith. Cordell Hull, erstwhile senator from Tennessee, had some regional political strength and a quality of dogged persistence that made him the longest-serving secretary of state (nearly twelve years) in American history, but by no stretch of the imagination was he a commanding figure in that role. He was mainly interested in the promotion of free trade, which in the decade of Hitler, Mussolini, Franco, and Japanese aggression, and then in the years of World War II, made him only marginally relevant to American foreign-policy decision making. There was no doubt that, throughout the Roosevelt administration, the White House and not the State Department was where key decisions were taken. That suited Roosevelt very well.

For secretary of the treasury he had wanted Carter Glass, senator from Virginia, whose seniority at the age of seventy-four was as unchallengeable as his ambitions were limited. Glass preferred to stay in the Senate, so Roosevelt turned instead to William H. Woodin, whose main political credentials were that he had given an early $10,000 to the FDR campaign and was thought to be a good link with big business. His health did not stand up to the job for long, which left Roosevelt exposed to two financial puritans: the assistant secretary, Dean Acheson, later to be a great secretary of state under Truman but at that stage rather a stiff-necked man in his thirties who resigned in the autumn of 1933 against FDR's manipulation of the price of gold, a backdoor method of devaluing the dollar; and Lewis Douglas, the director of the budget, who was at least as rigid for economy as Hoover had been, and who also resigned in protest ten months after FDR's inaugural. In the meantime Henry Morgenthau, Jr., Roosevelt's friend and Hudson Valley neighbor, became secretary of the treasury and served FDR faithfully to the end, although in 1944 he came up with the foolish scheme to reduce postwar Germany to a pastoral economy.

Of the other "regular" Democrats there were the two service chiefs: George Dern as secretary of war and Claude Swanson as secretary of the navy. Dern had the distinction of being a non-Mormon who had achieved the governorship of Utah, but his knowledge of — or even interest in — the army was distinctly limited. As soon as the reality of war loomed, Roosevelt replaced him with Stimson. Swanson was a senator from Virginia and did know something about the navy, having been chairman of the Senate Committee on Naval Affairs when Roosevelt was assistant secretary, but as this experience implies he was past the age of dynamism and certainly not a challenge for the future. As secretary of commerce, the president appointed Daniel C. Roper of South Carolina, whose history of regular Democratic service went far back: he had been assistant postmaster general at the beginning of the Wilson presidency. In place of the expired Walsh, Roosevelt appointed Homer S. Cummings of Connecticut as U.S. attorney general. Cummings had a high reputation as a prosecuting lawyer and was a man of strong Democratic record, but once again hardly a dynamic force.

The most interesting of Roosevelt's Democratic Cabinet appointments was Frances Perkins as secretary of labor. She, like several others, had been a Republican (and then a Bull Mooser) in the far-off days of Uncle Ted, but had worked for so long in association with Democrats in Albany, under both the Smith and FDR regimes, that the earlier affiliation had been scrubbed off. She was the first woman Cabinet officer in American history, and her appointment was made the more remarkable because she headed a department where male chauvinism might have been expected to be rampant. If the labor union leaders could not have one of their own there, they at least expected to be spared the infliction of a rather bossy female social worker. However, Perkins proved one of the most successful of Roosevelt's choices, earning almost universal respect, remaining right to the end, and establishing just the right relationship with the president, neither too close nor too distant, and always able to speak her mind. She was frequently referred to as Madame Perkins, which rather summed up these qualities. It matched Louis Howe often being called Colonel Howe, an interesting echo of Colonel House, Woodrow Wilson's old confidant, although it was not clear what military battalions either of them had ever commanded. The retention of "Ambassador," "Governor," and "Secretary," many years after the individuals concerned have ceased to hold such appointments, suggests that the liking for titles does not entirely disappear in a republic.

The nominal Republicans were more interesting than the Democrats, Frances Perkins apart. There was Henry Wallace, half a homespun farmer from Iowa and half a patrician dogmatist, lacking in political accommodations but always his own man, with some style but in a somewhat clodhopping mode, perhaps appropriate to his provenance. His father had preceded him as secretary of agriculture under Harding and then Coolidge and was the proprietor of *Wallace's Farmer*, a profitable journal with an influence far beyond Iowa. Roosevelt had originally wanted Morgenthau rather than Wallace for Agriculture, but he eventually decided it was wiser to give Iowa priority over the Hudson Valley in this post, and soon got the best of both worlds, for within little more than a year he had Morgenthau in the still more important position of secretary of the treasury. And Roosevelt warmed to Wallace, although never making him an intimate, to the extent of giving him the vice presidential slot for the 1940 election. After one term, he quietly dropped him in favor of Harry Truman, thereby saving the Western world — at any rate, in the judgment of the conventional wisdom — from the dangers of a Wallace presidency as the Allied victory turned into the Cold War. Wallace's 1933 appointment was, however, clearly an interesting, even a daring one.

Harold Ickes, a Chicago radical, was the second nominal Republican, but as he had been the Illinois organizer of Uncle Ted's

Bull Moose campaign in 1912 he obviously took his political affiliation fairly lightly. He was surprised but delighted when Roosevelt (after the job had been turned down by two senators) offered him the Department of the Interior. He was a formidably gruff personality, very successful at defending his own turf, and was widely known as "the old curmudgeon." His diaries provide an insight, well molded to his character, into the domestic policy life of the Roosevelt administration. In some ways analogously with Frances Perkins, he was a powerful and successful Cabinet officer who stayed the full term in the same job, like her partly because he was loyal but kept his distance and never got too embroiled in the White House. He also had the advantage that on many of the issues with which his department dealt — very different from those of a European minister of the interior: conservation, natural resources, national parks, forestry — Roosevelt was as instinctively radical as he was himself.

With these exceptions it was not an exciting Cabinet, giving the impression that it had been chosen with more regard to geographical balance, and perhaps also with some feeling that Roosevelt did not want much challenge to his own authority, than with a relentless search for quality. With it, fortified of course by a number of important assistants in the White House and in the departments, Roosevelt had to confront the most formidable threats to face any president since Lincoln.

Under the shadow of the financial crisis, with runs on banks across the country and failures every day, the presidency began in a swirl of activity. There may be room for dispute as to the extent to which the White House circle knew what they were doing. But there can be none about the pace of activity. Legislative proposals and executive actions poured out. And the bills all passed Congress, mostly by very strong majorities. Roosevelt had not only won the presidency but had scored strong Democratic majorities in both houses. The Senate was 62–34 Democratic and the House 313–119. Of course not all southern Democrats were progressives, but few Democratic members of the Congress wanted to fall out with Roosevelt at that stage, and many supported him out of political conviction and not merely regional provenance; Henry Rainey of Illinois was the first northern Democrat to be chosen Speaker of the House in more than fifty years. Furthermore, Congress was frightened by fear of the collapse of the American economy, and thus not disposed to resist the demands of a newly elected president who showed any route to recovery. In consequence, Roosevelt's threat in his inaugural speech to govern, if need be, by plenary executive power was as otiose in the period immediately following its delivery as it was unenforceable when the emergency had receded, Congress had regained some of its self-confidence, and special powers might have been useful. But between early March and mid-June 1933, the so-called hundred days, Congress passed anything sent up to it. And a vast proliferation of bills was enacted. Sometimes, indeed, the legislators went too far for the executive. Senator Hugo Black of Alabama, later a liberal member of the Supreme Court in spite of an embarrassing accusation of earlier Ku Klux Klan affiliation, proposed limiting work to five six-hour days and carried this proposition through the Senate by 56 votes to 30. The president, always commanding vivid homely metaphors, had to remind them that "hours have to be adapted to the rhythm of a cow."

The immediate issue, which had to be

faced on the Sunday following the Saturday inauguration, was the lancing of the boil of the banking crisis. Quite how this was done remains something of a mystery. Hoover, in his last days, had presumptuously called on Roosevelt to restore confidence by jettisoning most of the prospectus he had put forward during the campaign. In fact, the system was only too anxious to bound back if given half an opportunity. And the Emergency Banking Bill provided the impetus. It passed through the House and the Senate in one day without even a printed copy, and was available for signature in the White House that evening. The demoralization of the Republican opposition was illustrated by their minority leader in the House, who explained their acquiescence by saying: "The house is burning down and the President of the United States says this is the way to put out the fire." There was a temporary atmosphere of camaraderie, which was to find an echo during the London Blitz nearly eight years later. People even half enjoyed the inconvenience of not being able to get cash, headed by Eleanor Roosevelt, who did not know how they would manage to pay their bill at the Mayflower Hotel, where they had been installed on the threshold of their entry into the White House. In such an atmosphere any confidence-giving gestures, at which Roosevelt was superb, got a ready response.

The combination of Roosevelt's smile, a national bank holiday, and emergency bank legislation enabled confidence to flow back into the system, and when the obligatory closure came to an end after the following weekend most banks, given a certificate of health under the new legislation, were able to reopen and trade normally. The process was aided by Roosevelt giving the first of his wide-ranging press conferences on March 8, and the first of his series of broadcast Fireside Chats on March 14. There could be dissimulation in the background, but in the foreground the keynote of the new administration was openness and the exuding of confidence.

There followed such a rush of legislative activity and creation of new agencies as had never previously been seen. The Civilian Conservation Corps was the first creation, through Congress by March 31. What it essentially did was to set a number of the young unemployed to tidy up forests and national parks, living in camps and paid only a dollar a day. The Corps was run by the army, which made the "Civilian" in its name somewhat ironic, and it was attacked from the left for being too militaristic; Norman Thomas, the perennial socialist candidate for president (he had polled 884,000 votes in 1932), for whom Roosevelt nevertheless had considerable respect, thought they looked fascist rather than socialist. Nonetheless they had enrolled a quarter of a million young men by June, and the scheme, unlike some of the New Deal's other early ventures, survived until 1942 when, thanks to the war, there were virtually no unemployed left to enroll. It was the sort of enterprise that easily aroused Roosevelt's full backing. He believed in tidying up the countryside, even when it was as vast as that of the United States, and he did not like to see people standing about idle.

Next came the Agricultural Adjustment Act, or AAA, which was law by mid-May, at just about the same time as the setting up of the Tennessee Valley Authority. The AAA was designed to bring some order into agricultural markets, where surpluses had been heavily deflating prices and turning the terms of trade in favor of industrial consumers and against farming producers. It had many of the features of the much-maligned European Common

Agricultural Policy, which came into being a quarter of a century later. Surpluses were taken off the market by the device of paying farmers not to raise the staple products of wheat, cotton, hogs, and tobacco. This was effective but appeared perverse, particularly as many Americans were still undernourished. It also had the effect of putting most federal money into the hands of big and relatively rich farmers, who had more capacity for "not raising hogs." But, like Europe's CAP, it did something to redress the balance in favor of the countryside, and it did mitigate the near despair to which many farmers had been reduced.

The Tennessee Valley Authority sounds local but was in fact a vast scheme of regional development in one of the poorest parts of the United States. The Tennessee River loops through seven states — Virginia, North Carolina, Kentucky, Tennessee, Georgia, Alabama, and Mississippi. The area involved was a third the size of Britain and was one of deep rural poverty. Flooding was frequent, malaria was rampant, and only 3 percent of the farmyards had electricity. It was an area tailor-made for Roosevelt's progressiveness. Unlike the British politician who was described as being "a socialist in every department but his own," FDR was at his most radical in the areas about which he knew most, public (electric) power and the rural economy. The overture from that forbidding-sounding but curiously esteemed modern opera *The Electrification of the Soviet Union*, with the USSR transformed into the USA, would have been a more natural theme song for FDR than Al Smith's unfortunate "Sidewalks of New York." The legislation authorizing the TVA was law by May 18, 1933, and this vast project, although not without a few inevitable hiccups, was on balance a major long-term success.

Roosevelt was indeed accused of introducing a massive piece of regional "socialization," and Representative Joseph Martin of Massachusetts, who was later to achieve considerable fame as a target for brilliant presidential raillery — Martin, Barton, and Fish — in Roosevelt's 1940 campaign, thought it followed a Communist pattern. Roosevelt handled these charges with typical aplomb. "I'll tell them it [TVA] is neither fish nor fowl, but whatever it is it will taste awful good to the people of the Tennessee Valley." The TVA aroused the cross-party enthusiasm of notable western progressives, such as the Republican senator and liberal hero George W. Norris of

Nebraska. Their instinctive isolationism (not shared in the 1930s by Norris) presented no problems until the late 1930s, and they hitched themselves to the Roosevelt bandwagon, which was still moving impressively along.

The progress of the bandwagon was lubricated by the generally popular (although not with Eleanor Roosevelt) repeal of Prohibition as it concerned wine and beer. This was partly disguised as a budget-balancing measure (although it needed little dissimulation), for the government took a useful cut on the newly legalized libations. Hard liquor took some time officially to follow suit, but the walls of the citadel were irrevocably breached, and by late June FDR, on holiday at Campobello, was heavily rebuked by Eleanor for "mixing a cocktail" for their youngest son, then aged seventeen. It is difficult to make a cocktail out of beer and wine, and had the president been acting illegally as well as, in his wife's view, irresponsibly, her rebuke would surely have been even more crushing. Fortunately for him, Campobello is in Canada.

The budget-balancing promises rashly offered in Pittsburgh during the campaign troubled certain quarters. The defense budget was cut from $752 million a year to $531 million (the latter figure would hardly have paid for one Stealth bomber at today's prices), with the bulk of the cuts falling on the army. This led to General MacArthur indulging in a somewhat hysterical face-to-face confrontation with Roosevelt, which was the beginning of his alienation from Democratic presidents and culminated in his sacking by Truman eighteen years later. Federal government salaries were generally cut, and the poor bonus seekers, so far from getting their bonuses, found that veterans' invalid allowances, which admittedly had been something of a racket, were reduced by $400 million. At the same time, new financial commitments, for the CCC, the AAA, the TVA, and other specific projects, were being freely entered into. There was a certain half-sensible logic about what was being done, corresponding to a sort of stumbling Keynesianism, which characterized the early actions of the administration. As, however, Keynes did not publish his *General Theory of Employment, Interest and Money* until early 1936, it would be a mistake to regard his formula of — to put it very crudely — governments spending their way out of depressions as a fully coherent doctrine in Cambridge, England, at this stage, let alone in Washington for the early New Deal. Keynes had, however, made a moderately rewarding call upon Roosevelt in the White House in the summer of 1934, when his ideas were already far advanced. But many people overestimated the amount of agreement they had reached with the president in similar meetings.

The most compendious, most controversial, and maybe the most important of the early New Deal measures came toward the end of the hundred days. The National Industrial Recovery bill was presented to Congress in mid-May 1933 and became law on June 16, when it went through the Senate by the unusually narrow majority for those days of 46 to 39, with, as a mildly sinister omen, eleven Democrats voting against. Some would say that the National Industrial Recovery Act was not just compendious but a ragbag. Eager youngish men, enjoying the heady atmosphere of new power in Washington, managed to get their various pet projects inserted into its spread of provisions. Two main lines of policy were discernible. First, business was allowed to become more corporate. Competition might be a fine watchword in conditions of prosperity, when it determined who got to the top of the pile fastest; it was less attractive in conditions of adversity, when it dragged everyone down into unprofitable undercutting in shrinking markets. Title I of NIRA was something of a trade associations' charter. It turned its back on the Progressive tradition — embraced by Uncle Ted — of trust-busting and hostility to cartels. As such it never carried the support of liberals such as the Supreme Court justice Louis Brandeis, who believed in the distribution, not the concentration, of power. It also offended some of the normally progressive western senators, which partly accounted for the weak majority in their chamber. This lurch toward corporatism was symbolized by the "Blue Eagle" device for businesses willing to cooperate in a government-organized attempt to restore national prosperity. If they accepted a code that involved eschewing price cutting, paying a minimum wage of $12 for a forty-hour week (not a munificent sum, even by 1933 standards), they were allowed to display the bird on and around their products. Some, who were skeptical, referred to it as the Blue Buzzard, but most of the frightened business community accepted it. The automobile industry presented a fairly typical example.

Chevrolet (which became the core of General Motors) accepted it, but Henry Ford, who paid higher wages than the qualifying floor, rejected it contumaciously.

There were other complications. Hugh Johnson, an erstwhile brigadier general of cavalry, was appointed to head the scheme. He was thought to have the imprimatur of Bernard Baruch, under whom he had worked in World War I. But Baruch, a substantial contributor to Democratic funds, influential in Washington, and an old friend of Winston Churchill's, was not a man with whom to hunt butterflies, let alone tigers. He was soon denigrating Johnson, and maybe rightly. Johnson was dynamic, slightly drunken, and megalomaniacal. In some but not all respects he was a suitable partner across the industrial divide for John L. Lewis, the mine workers' leader, who also erupted onto the national scene at about this time. Johnson started with great panache, and for a time achieved almost more publicity than Roosevelt himself. This is always a dangerous position for a subordinate, and it brought about the brigadier's almost inevitable downfall. It resulted first in the Public Works Administration, the main creation of Title II of NIRA, being entrusted not to

Johnson but to Ickes, the secretary of the interior. Roosevelt did this because he feared that Johnson's wild and flailing methods of administration would provide very lax control over the $3.3 billion of public money involved. The PWA was a serious matter. Among the projects completed under its auspices were the Triborough Bridge in New York, the linking of Key West with mainland Florida, the building of Boulder Dam on the Colorado River, and the modernization of the New York–Washington railroad link, as well as innumerable courthouses, hospitals, and schools throughout the nation. All of this was done, with increasingly hostile press and business communities watching hawk-eyed from the sidelines, without any serious suggestion of fraud or even financial carelessness; this showed the wisdom of Roosevelt's decision to entrust such expenditure to Ickes's careful and slow nitpicking rather than to Johnson's flamboyance.

Implementing that decision caused the newly elected and, at the time, almost all-powerful president such anguish that he could not do it face-to-face but only in a meeting of the full Cabinet, which Johnson was exceptionally attending. Here it was presented under a camouflage of great praise for Johnson and with the excuse that it was necessary to free his exceptional talents from the burdens of the bureaucracy of Title II in order that he might concentrate upon the flair-requiring tasks of Title I. Johnson was not taken in, and reacted sufficiently strongly for Roosevelt to get Frances Perkins to take him for a two-hour drive to calm him down and prevent his resigning. For the moment it worked, but not to much avail, for in August 1934, fourteen months later, Johnson's increasingly erratic behavior made Roosevelt want his resignation. Once again, he avoided the direct encounter. The faithful Frances Perkins and Donald Richberg, counsel to the National Recovery Administration, were called in to assist at the execution. Quite why Roosevelt thought their presence would make it less painful, either for the beheaded or for himself as the executioner, is not clear, but it was an interesting example of the methods of operation of the man who for nearly a decade and a half exercised a greater mixture of charm, serpentine method, and beneficial power than anyone else in the democratic world.

NRA had a variety of impacts upon the national environment, the fortunes of individuals, and the fluctuating relationship of the New Deal with the business community before it was invalidated as being in restraint of trade on May 27, 1935. This was by a decision of the Supreme Court on what was known popularly as the Sick Chicken Case and in the annals of the law as *Schechter Poultry Corp. v. United States*, a title that gives the impression of an unequal contest. Nonetheless, the winner was David rather than Goliath.

Perhaps the longest-lasting impact of NIRA was contained in the originally little noticed Section 7(a) of Title I. This put the authority of the federal government behind the right of workers to organize and bargain collectively. It led to John L. Lewis putting out, within two weeks of the NIRA becoming law, a poster with a picture of FDR and the caption "The President Wants You to Join the Union." "The Union" was the United Mine Workers, and the posters were mostly exhibited in the soft-coal fields of Pennsylvania and West Virginia. In the former state alone, they quickly yielded 128,000 new members. As both states were areas of captive mines (owned by the big steel companies), there followed a degree of confrontation with some of the most traditionally antiunion corporations in America. There was a further complication, which was that Myron C. Taylor, the head of U.S. Steel (the market leader), had also something of a special relationship with Roosevelt, of whom he apparently kept a picture (although accompanied by one of Mussolini) in his office. Nor was the admiration only one-way: in 1940, FDR was to make Taylor his ambassador to the Vatican, a highly trusted listening post in Italy.

Even such a sophisticated and politically mobile businessman as Taylor, however, would not give in without a struggle; 35,000 Pennsylvania miners went out on strike before the issue was settled, in favor of the full recognition of the union. Roosevelt managed to get Taylor and a few of his lesser tycoon companions to attend a White House conference with Lewis, when the president abjured them all to behave like a family. If they did, the family was a severely dysfunctional one, although Lewis, who had everything to gain, was trying to be like a benevolent uncle.

Nevertheless, it was a considerable triumph for Roosevelt, given the previous arrogance of American business leaders, to get the meeting to take place at all, and it coincided with several high-water marks. First, it marked the apogee of Lewis's relationship with Roosevelt. Rather like Huey Long, governor of and sometime senator from Louisiana, he was too self-obsessed to be able to continue a satisfactory junior partnership, and bitterly opposed FDR's re-election in 1940. For less flamboyant union leaders, however, particularly those in the automobile and clothing industries, Section 7(a) laid a foundation of loyalty of labor to Roosevelt, which, according to some commentators, determined the whole course of American politics by making the Democrats the dominant party in the electorate at least until the end of the Truman presidency, maybe even through to the Kennedy and Johnson years.

At the end of the strenuous congressional special session in 1933, Roosevelt retired to Campobello with the feeling that he had made the legislative branch work harder, and more submissively to the White House, than it had ever done before. Senators and representatives went home with similar satisfaction, but maybe also feeling that a little more independence might be necessary in the future. That summer of 1933 was also the cusp of the president's changing and deteriorating relations with business leaders. At the time of Roosevelt's election and inauguration, they were seriously frightened. They were prepared to cling to any lifeboat. But as conditions improved they wanted, above all, to regain their self-confidence and national esteem. They attached almost more importance to this than to their money, although few of them became seriously short of that.

A key occasion in 1933, comparable with Roosevelt's requiring the steel masters to meet on equal terms with Lewis, was the summoning before the Senate Committee on Banking and Currency of John Pierpont Morgan, for whom the New York financial community had hitherto almost amounted to an independent kingdom. It was the equivalent, *mutatis* and a good deal *mutandis,* of the pope being asked to explain the Vatican investment policy before a committee of the Italian parliament. Morgan did not cut a good figure. When asked why he had paid no income tax for the previous three years, he replied that he did not know and that it was a matter for his accountant.

The significant thing was that Morgan came at all. The gods were reducing themselves to the ranks of mortals. And they hated doing so. It was their public regard even more than the margins of their fortunes that they resented losing. This is what Roosevelt declined to restore. The caricature of the tycoon who is saved from drowning but abuses his rescuers for not having retrieved his top hat is brilliantly apposite. (Curiously, Churchill, whose oratory was normally much more high-flown than Roosevelt's, was to use a variant of this metaphor — the headgear had become a schoolboy's cap rather than a tycoon's glossy hat — in a House of Commons debate immediately after one of his wartime visits to Roosevelt ten years later.) Already by the turn of 1933–34 the worst fears with which Roosevelt had started were eased. The banking crisis had been surmounted — perhaps more by luck than by judgment — and the economy was showing hesitant but encouraging signs of recovery. The industrial production index picked up strongly over the summer of 1933, but then stayed on a plateau. Unemployment fell from 15 million to 11 million. This was enough for resentment to replace fear as the dominant emotion in most of those from Roosevelt's own social background. They quickly came to regard him as a class traitor and to denounce him in private and semipublic in the most unmeasured terms. Their fury was not assuaged by the great success of the Democrats in the November 1934 mid-term elections. Contrary to the traditional pattern, the preponderance of the Democrats in both chambers became even greater. In the House they advanced from 313 to 322 seats (out of a total of 432), and in the Senate they picked up another 9, advancing to 69 as against 27 Republicans. This sweeping vote of confidence merely made the administration's opponents add demagoguery and vote buying to the sins of the New Deal.

Just as the economy, although well off the floor of 1932–33, faltered and failed to achieve a performance that took it back to the boom years of the 1920s, so did some of Roosevelt's fair-weather friends of the first year get off the bandwagon. This was not merely a question of Grotonians, Harvard classmates, Hudson Valley neighbors, leaders of Wall Street, and members of the Knickerbocker Club. Two of his most populist supporters, neither of whom it would have been possible to imagine in any of these affiliations, moved into enmity. The first was Huey Long and the second was Father Charles Coughlin, the radio priest from Detroit, who commanded vast audiences. Coughlin began so enthusiastically that, with doubtful theological validity, he proclaimed the New Deal to be "Christ's deal." Long, who believed, not without an element of truth, that he had been the crucial agent of FDR's securing the Democratic nomination in 1932, and in the early days of the new presidency believed that he deserved high consideration as a result, made the mistake of thinking that he could subsequently patronize Roosevelt.

This was a ludicrous miscalculation, for if ever there was a man not to be patronized it was FDR. In a disastrous visit to the White House in 1934, Long kept his straw hat on in the Oval Office except occasionally to give the president an admonitory tap on the knee with it. Thereafter the Kingfish was in outer darkness, and few tears were shed in the White House when he was shot dead in Baton Rouge in September 1935. That disposed of the threat that he would emerge as a third-party candidate in the presidential election of 1936. Roosevelt did not fear that Long could win, but he did fear the same kind of damage that Uncle Ted had done to Taft in 1912.

There were still two other possible threats of this sort left. There was Father Coughlin, whose switch to an anti-Roosevelt position had done nothing to impair the enthusiasm of his audiences. In retrospect, considering the initial difficulties that John F. Kennedy had nearly thirty years later in persuading the American electorate that, as a contemporary joke put it, his actual father in Boston was more of a danger than his spiritual father in Rome, it is difficult to believe that a soutane-encrusted Catholic priest could have been much of a menace in the mid-1930s. The other threat was Dr. Francis Townsend, a patient-popular Californian general practitioner, who decided in late 1933 that millenarian politics were more interesting than diagnosis and propounded a scheme by which both the health of the economy and social justice would be advanced by the federal government giving everyone over sixty a free pension of $150, later raised to $200 a month. The sums, even in 1930s value, were not astronomical — they would hardly have enticed a J. P. Morgan or a William Randolph Hearst — but they were enough to have destroyed any budgetary prudence and to offer a promised land to many of the impoverished elderly as well as to those who approached old age with apprehension. It was perhaps fortunate for the containment of this appeal that the age structure of the population was not then as back-end-loaded as it is today. Nevertheless, the popularity of Townsend's appeal spread rapidly, by no means only in California, but at least as far east as Chicago: there a convention of his "Old Age Pension" clubs seemed to favor a third-party strategy, to which, however, the doctor had the good sense to be opposed.

Roosevelt's reaction to these various bursts of opposition — invalidation from the Supreme Court, class hostility from the right, populist outflanking from the demagogues — was to launch a second wave of New Deal radicalism, in several ways more provocative than the first. At the end of January 1935, he lost his proposition that the United States should adhere to the World Court of International Justice. Thirty-six senators voted against: enough, even if by a margin of only four, to withhold the necessary two-thirds majority. It was a blow, both because Roosevelt was unused to being defeated and because he had thought it would be a satisfactory halfway house between bringing the United States into the League of Nations (which he saw as beyond his political capacity) and doing nothing for internationalism (which would have let down many, not least Eleanor Roosevelt). In early 1935, Roosevelt was perceived as being in a low mood — unusual with him, whatever were the objective circumstances. He was described as being "peevish, restless, even indecisive."* The odd word in this description is "even," for Roosevelt while rarely peevish or restless was frequently indecisive, particularly while hovering over a problem before swooping into a delayed decision. In that January, however, he had several reasons for being indecisive.

The components of the second New Deal, which was also the prelude to the 1936 campaign for reelection, were broadly the following: first, the National Labor Relations Act, which enabled the famous 7(a) of the NIRA to live again, even though the parent law had been struck down by the Supreme Court; second, the Social Security Act, which in old-age pensions and unemployment benefits brought to America most of the modest safety nets that Asquith, Lloyd George, and Winston Churchill had introduced to Britain in the pre-1914 Liberal govern-

*James MacGregor Burns and Susan Dunn, *The Three Roosevelts: Patrician Leaders Who Transformed America* (New York: Atlantic Monthly Press, 2001), p. 288.

ment; third, the Banking Act of 1935, which reorganized the Federal Reserve Board and generally strengthened federal powers of supervision to an extent that aroused the strong opposition of Senator Carter Glass, whom Roosevelt had mistakenly wanted to make his secretary of the treasury in 1933; fourth, the Public Utility Holding Company Act, which substantially weakened the power of the great electrical conglomerations, in many ways the 1930s equivalent of the 1900s railroad trusts, and which helped to make Wendell Willkie, FDR's otherwise liberal 1940 opponent, into a Republican; fifth, the appropriation of $5 million for the Works Progress Administration, which was life after death for an earlier work relief program, the Civil Works Administration, and, with Harry Hopkins in charge of the reincarnation, a peculiarly vigorous one; sixth, and most important and most provocative (to Roosevelt haters) of the lot, the Revenue Act of 1935. This raised surtax rates on high incomes, increased estate and gift taxes, and also subjected corporate profits, whether distributed or undistributed, to higher rates. And it was not done apologetically, with any suggestion that the punishment, necessary only because of economic stringency, hurt the president even more than it hurt the recipients. On the contrary, FDR proposed the legislation by announcing that "great accumulations of wealth cannot be justified on the basis of personal and family security."

The period 1935–36 marked a distinct break point in Roosevelt's attitudes and strategy. During his first two years in the White House, his course was that of consensus, bipartisanship, and trying to placate all major groups and classes. He wanted as many as possible to be within the Rooseveltian tent. After the climacteric, to which about equal contributions were made by the Supreme Court striking down the NRA and by the increasing hostility toward him of the eastern establishment from which he had sprung, he became less inclusive. Of course, he wanted a secure majority still to be within the tent — an aim he abundantly achieved in November 1936. But he moved from his previous all-inclusiveness to a view that some well-chosen enemies might actually be a help in underpinning the enthusiasm of the majority.

There were two key manifestations of this new spirit. The first was his reaction to the invalidation of NRA. There was no doubt that it hurt him, particularly, perhaps, because the famous liberal justices Louis Brandeis and Benjamin Cardozo had joined with the predictable conservatives to make the decision of the Supreme Court unanimous. He denounced it at a press conference four days later in a statement lasting nearly an hour and a half that reads more like an alternative and higher judgment than a political refutation. He rejected the Court's narrow interpretation of the Interstate Commerce Clause, upon which its decision was based. This narrowness of interpretation, he insisted in the most resonant phrase of his exposition, put America back into the "horse-and-buggy days" (that particular phrase was perhaps more political than judicial). This extended press conference, and associated events, paved the way to two destinations, the route beginning in the same direction but subsequently forking. The first was epitomized by his speech to a packed crowd in Madison Square Garden, New York, almost at the end of the 1936 campaign.

"For twelve years this nation was afflicted with hear-nothing, see-nothing, do-nothing government. . . . Nine mocking years of the golden calf and three long years of the scourge! Nine long years at the ticker [tape] and three long years in the breadlines. Nine mad years of mirage and three long years of despair!" Powerful forces, he continued, were trying to bring back the doctrine "that government is best which is most indifferent. . . . Never before in our history have these forces been so united against one candidate as they stand today. They are unanimous in their hate for me — *and I welcome their hatred.* . . . I should like to have it said of my first administration that in it the forces of self-ishness and lust for power *met their match.* I should like to have it said of my second administration that in it these forces *met their master."*

It was quite a different note from any that he struck in his 1932 campaign. Then, all were to be conciliated. Now a (powerful) minority were to be provoked in order to make the majority more enthusiastic. The tactic worked brilliantly. The result of the 1936 presidential election exceeded all possible Democratic hopes. The Republicans put up a thoroughly moderate candidate in the shape of Alfred M. Landon, the governor of Kansas, who had been a Bull Mooser in 1912 and whose vice presidential running mate was the liberal Chicago publisher

Frank Knox, another 1912 supporter of Uncle Ted, whom Roosevelt was to make his secretary of the navy at the same time that he made Stimson secretary of war, when European events forced him to treat these two Cabinet offices as administratively serious rather than as politically convenient. Nor was the third-party threat eliminated. Father Coughlin found a surrogate in William Lemke, a North Dakota congressman. Norman Thomas continued to plow his lone Socialist furrow, and there were miscellaneous Communist and Prohibitionist candidates as well. Roosevelt simply annihilated them all. He won 61 percent of the vote. He confined the populist Lemke to under a million votes. He reduced the personally esteemed Thomas from 800,000 in 1932 to under 200,000. With more central significance, he confined Landon to carrying only the states of Vermont and Maine. It was the most sweeping victory since the earliest days of the Republic, and it was achieved against an overwhelmingly hostile press. In the forty-six states that voted for Roosevelt he had very little newspaper support. Even more was the victory achieved against the wishes of those who regarded themselves as the natural leaders of American opinion.

Some Democrats — for instance, Al Smith and at least 80 percent of the old upper class, Roosevelt's own — voted solidly against him. But their opinions and votes counted for little against the solid support of blue-collar, farm-state (Landon could not even carry his home state of Kansas), and lower-middle-class America. It was the first fairly rigid class election in American history, and it was at once paradoxical and typical of many such contests throughout the world that the champion of the sansculottes should have been the most upper-class president since George Washington.

Such an overwhelming victory obviously carried with it the seeds of hubris, and this indeed proved to be the case. FDR was sworn in for his second term on January 20, 1937, the first time that an inaugural had been brought forward from March 4; the change of date was in itself a repudiation of the horse-and-buggy days. Presidents no longer needed four months to get from their front porches to Washington. It was a day of cold, penetrating rain. And the ceremony was not joyous. Charles Evans Hughes, who swore him in, was one of the most political — and Republican — of chief justices. He had been the GOP candidate against Wilson in 1916. He had been secretary of state in the administrations of Harding and Coolidge. Both he and Roosevelt, as they faced each other, knew that they were in for major conflict. And the president chose to deliver an address that was not a bland congratulation on his first term and great victory, but a harsh challenge to the problems of the second term. "I see one-third of a nation ill-housed, ill-clad, ill-nourished. It is not in despair that I paint you that picture. I paint it for you in hope — because the nation, seeing and understanding the injustice in it, proposes to paint it out."

And the first thing that, in Roosevelt's view, had to be painted out was the blocking power of Hughes and his eight (mostly elderly) associate justices. The president waited only another seventeen days before launching his "Court-packing plan," which was meant to remove, or at least greatly to modify, their blocking power. It was bold, but it was to lead to his greatest defeat, and to launch the second term, in spite of the splendor of the electoral victory, on a path of frustration.

5

Setbacks: Political and Economic

The greatest political defeat of Roosevelt's career was his ham-fisted attempt in the first half of 1937 to reform (some would say to subjugate) the Supreme Court of the United States. He sent a message to Congress arguing disingenuously that the Supreme Court could not keep up with its work and that efficient administration called for the appointment of an additional justice for each justice aged seventy or over. His defeat was rich in paradox. First, it followed so closely his great triumph of the previous November. Second, in the five-month battle, which raged from February to July, Roosevelt, the master politician, made mistake after mistake, while the "horse and buggy" Court, with its aged and obscurantist justices, played brilliantly its defensive hand. As a result, in a far from inevitable alliance with the Senate, it scuppered the most important early proposal of the recently and most powerfully reelected president in American history.

By the end of 1936, the justices had declared New Deal legislation unconstitutional in seven of the nine cases that had come before them. Roosevelt's exasperation, fortified by his electoral triumph, was wholly understandable, but his tactics were execrable. On February 3, 1937, he gave the traditional White House dinner for the justices, but he did not even hint to them what he was planning. Two days later he announced his proposals to the Cabinet, who took them sycophantically, and to the congressional leaders, who were much less inclined to go along. Vice President Garner was equally unenthusiastic. So were several others, including the chairman of the House Judiciary Committee and, perhaps most important of the lot, Senator Burton K. Wheeler of Montana, who for the previous four years had been one of the most reliable of New Deal supporters but who did not like the Court bill. He was further alienated by a crude semibribe attempt by Tommy "the Cork" Corcoran, who, bouncing around on Capitol Hill with all the overenthusiasm of a young White House aide, offered Wheeler the opportunity to influence the choice of one or two new Supreme Court justices if he went along. This was rather the equivalent of offering Charles de Gaulle a few military medals if he acceded to Anglo-Saxon hegemony, and needless to say, it had a similar counterproductive effect. The seriousness of the revolt lay in the fact that the most vocal opponents were Democrats — the Republicans hardly counted in this battle — who Roosevelt thought had been elected on his coattails, which increased both his exasperation and his tactlessness.

It was not that the opponents of the Court-packing plan did not see the existence of a problem. They did not expect Roosevelt just to lie down under the 1935–36 massacre of his legislation. It was more that they thought his method ill-chosen and, an amazing criticism of the master politician, lacking in subtlety. They also resented his failure to consult with Congress. As a result the forces of reform were quickly in disarray. Those of resistance, on the other hand, were skillfully marshaled. The justices drastically reduced their degree of exposure. Between March 29 and May 24, 1937, they upheld a minimum-wage law in the state of Washington, a farm mortgage act, and the collective bargaining provisions of the Railroad Labor Act. Then they put the icing on the cake by upholding the National Labor Relations Act and the Social Security Act. It could be held that this wave of "progressive" decisions owed more to political tactics than to the rigors of legal logic, for a number of them contradicted the earlier ones. Nonetheless, they took a good deal of the wind out of Roosevelt's sails. They were accompanied by a shrewd counterattack on the weakest point in the president's front. He had made the mistake of giving a false reason for his plan. He said that judicial waiting lists ought to be reduced, and in the course of deploying this argument suggested that elderly justices were slow if not incompetent as well. This was hardly likely to propitiate either the chief justice (who was seventy-five and probably unpropitiable in any event) or Brandeis (eighty and the oldest member, but in general liberal). The "false reason" further backfired when Chief Justice Hughes, supported by Brandeis and a conservative associate justice, Willis Van Devanter, released to the Senate Judiciary Committee a statement that the Court was fully abreast of its work, and that more justices would mean more delay.

On May 18, that committee, despite its large Democratic majority, voted by 10 to

8 that the bill not pass. On the same day Van Devanter resigned, thereby giving Roosevelt his first opportunity to make a Supreme Court nomination, for throughout his first term all nine justices had been both healthily long-lived and stubbornly unretiring. The irony was that there is some evidence that not only Van Devanter but George Sutherland, also a conservative justice, would have been glad to retire earlier had Roosevelt's own Economy Act of 1933 not reduced the lifetime salary of retired justices from $20,000 to $10,000. A generous Supreme Court pension bill, which would have passed without difficulty, might have assured the president of most of what he wanted without driving the Court plan to its fall. And it was a very considerable fall, which from at least May onward had become inevitable. He had promised the first Court vacancy to Joseph T. Robinson of Arkansas, the Senate majority leader. Robinson was very keen to move to the Court. (It was indeed remarkable, the beacon of attraction that this high judicial appointment was for many senior politicians who happened also to have been lawyers of moderate distinction.) The promise to Robinson precluded a more imaginative appointment, but it kept him

locked in with Roosevelt on the Court issue. Robinson's Senate support became the more necessary for Roosevelt in mid-June, when Vice President Garner, who had never liked the Court plan, flounced off to Texas, leaving Robinson to bear the whole burden in the Senate. Within five weeks that burden killed him. On July 14, he was found dead on the floor of his Washington bathroom.

It was all part of the Greek tragedy aspect of the whole affair. With Robinson's death the Court bill also died, although Roosevelt took another four weeks to recognize the fact. In the meantime he got himself too embroiled in the election for a successor Senate majority leader. He wanted Alben Barkley of Kentucky (later to be Truman's running mate in the unexpectedly successful 1948 presidential election) rather than Pat Harrison of Mississippi, and he succeeded by one vote. But a lot of bruises were left. All of these Senate figures — Garner of Texas, Robinson of Arkansas, Harrison of Mississippi, Barkley of Kentucky — underlined how much of a southern and border-state affair that chamber, particularly in its Democratic manifestation, was in those days, and how carefully Roosevelt, even at the apogee of his power, needed to pick his way through its quicksand, which on the Court issue he signally, and surprisingly, failed to do. It was the era of the Democratic "Solid South," when Democratic majorities in Congress were dependent on relatively conservative (although mostly internationalist) southerners, with whom presidents had every reason to tread carefully, as FDR had done most of the time in his first term.

The second irony was that this unusually unavailing struggle of Roosevelt's quickly proved itself unnecessary. In place of Van Devanter he appointed the young senator Hugo Black. Then, in the next few years, Supreme Court vacancies occurred like November's falling leaves. The president was able to appoint his own solicitor general, Stanley Reed; Felix Frankfurter, a Harvard academic; William O. Douglas, an equally liberal Yale academic; Attorney General Frank Murphy; Senator James Byrnes of South Carolina, later to be Truman's not entirely satisfactory secretary of state; and Robert Jackson, Murphy's replacement as attorney general. By 1941 the only pre-Roosevelt appointments who remained were Harlan F. Stone (a liberal) and Owen Roberts. The paradoxical outcome of FDR's ill-fated Court venture was that he ended up with a Court that would no longer challenge his measures but with a Congress much more loath to pass them, at any rate in automatic response to the say-so of the White House.

The failure of the Supreme Court bill was far from being Roosevelt's only setback in what should have been years of opportunity and achievement following the triumph of 1936. There was little but bad news from the world across both the Atlantic and the Pacific Oceans, and there was nothing effective that Roosevelt felt that he could do about the passing of the stations of the road to World War II. In September 1935, Mussolini attacked Abyssinia and, despite some ineffective League of Nations sanctions, quickly conquered it. In March 1936, Hitler sent his troops into the demilitarized Rhineland. The Treaty of Versailles was thus effectively torn up, but France and Britain hesitated until the moment for any possible enforcement was past. In July of that year, a military revolt against Spain's newly elected Popular Front government quickly developed into a major civil war. Then, in the summer of 1937, which was the last year of relative calm in Europe, Japanese aggression in

China reerupted, leading to large-scale fighting and the occupation of Shanghai. In 1938, Hitler's adventures in Europe resumed, and with a new and stronger momentum. Austria was absorbed in March; the alleged grievances of the Sudeten-Deutsch against the Czech state were pushed to a crisis by Germany in May and again even more strongly in September, when a series of three meetings, all on German soil, between Neville Chamberlain and Hitler, and with Édouard Daladier of France and Mussolini being present at the final one, led to Western submission in the Munich agreement.

These successive crises left Roosevelt in an agony of impotence. His instincts were strongly antifascist. Privately he was much less equivocal about the Spanish Civil War than was Winston Churchill. Furthermore, he was a natural interventionist, one characteristic he shared with Uncle Ted. He believed in the benevolent power of the United States and in its duty to set the world to rights, as he had shown by his ardent support for Wilson in World War I. But he was also a consummate politician (even if he could occasionally make clanging mistakes, as with the Court bill), with almost too acute a sense of what was politically possible and what was not. He had a repugnance for moving too far ahead of public opinion, as he was constantly making clear to a sometimes exasperated Eleanor Roosevelt through his refusal to endorse her more utopian initiatives. And he was convinced — with some reason — that as the mid-thirties turned into the late thirties, both public and congressional opinion remained essentially isolationist. Sometimes, too, there were other, more specific inhibitions. The American Roman Catholic hierarchy was strongly on General Franco's side in the Spanish Civil War. With the 1936 presidential election, widely thought before its outcome to be hazardous, barely four months away when Franco started his revolt, Roosevelt believed that he would lose a large swath of the Catholic vote if he came out for the Republican government. Nothing in the later course of the Spanish conflict changed that view.

As a result of these various factors, Roosevelt over the period of 1936–38 played a faltering foreign policy hand. He moralized without effect, and his two most hyped foreign policy speeches bewildered more than they led. The first, at Chautauqua in New York State, a traditional sounding board for homilies, was before the 1936 election, and has already been referred to in chapter 1 in connection with FDR's somewhat excessive claims to personal experience of the horrors of war in 1917–18. That speech was far more in the genre of an antiwar novel of the 1920s than of a Churchillian anti-Nazi call to arms of the 1930s.

The second speech was delivered in Chicago in October 1937, when FDR made a triumphant drive through the city and then addressed an estimated crowd of 75,000. This was superficially a much harder speech than the Chautauqua one. It acknowledged the deteriorating world situation. It denounced a reign of terror and international lawlessness that seriously threatened the very foundations of civilization, declaring, "The peace-loving nations must make a concerted effort to quarantine the aggressor." This sounded more like a call to action, but asked at a subsequent press conference what he meant by it, Roosevelt gave a wholly obfuscating series of answers. So that, too, faded into vagueness.

Nor were matters, even apart from the Court-packing debacle, going well at home. For the economy began to exhibit symptoms of sickening in the autumn of 1937. There was a "black Tuesday" on Wall Street in October; unemployment climbed back above 10 million; steel production (the most sensitive indicator of the time) went into decline; and there was a real threat of conditions reverting almost to 1933 levels. By the spring of 1938, this setback was turning into a near catastrophe. Winston Churchill, who combined his greatness with a remarkable capacity for being one of the gullible Wall Street speculators, found himself as seriously embarrassed as in 1929. He prepared to sell Chartwell, not only his country retreat but also the essential base of his writing and political operations, and was saved only by the eleemosynary intervention of a South African rand millionaire.

In 1937–38, however, Roosevelt had much more to worry about in the consequences of the recession than its effect upon the private fortunes (even had he known of it) of his future wartime ally. The slump coincided, and to some extent caused, the nadir of his twelve-year presidency. This was mainly because he was totally torn as to how to cope with the recrudescence of the economic problems he thought he had put behind him in 1933–34. He was half persuaded by

Henry Morgenthau, who was not only his secretary of the treasury but also his closest friend in the Cabinet, that 1937 was the time to strike hard for a balanced budget. Yet the cutbacks in federal expenditure in that year were fairly clearly one of the causes of the recession. Roosevelt hovered for some months between two directly incompatible approaches. He was also plagued, at the end of 1937, by a seriously infected jaw, which dragged down his habitual vitality. To add to his troubles the temporary absence of political touch that had first been displayed in his handling of the Supreme Court continued to affect him. By the spring of 1938 he had not only had to give a good deal of ground on the Fair Labor Standards Act (the issue was, essentially, the demand of southern senators and representatives for a lower minimum wage in the South than in the North), but had also been effectively defeated on an executive branch reorganization bill. This he saw as an invasion of presidential territory. It was also an indication of how much he had temporarily mismanaged the separation-of-powers balance. In the Court-packing fiasco, he had been trying to invade judicial territory. To do so, he ought to have forged an executive-legislative alliance. It was, after all, the legislation of Congress that the Court had been busily engaged in overturning. But without this alliance secured in advance, he had to beat an ignominious retreat from judicial territory. He also found that he had driven a dividing shaft between the executive and the legislature, which spilled over into other issues. After the midterm elections of 1938, progressive legislation of the sort that appealed to most urban northern Democrats was to be stalled in Congress until Lyndon Johnson's outsized victory of 1964 swept forty extra northerners into the House.

During an early spring cure at Warm Springs, Roosevelt had at least made up his mind that a fairly massive further federal injection of purchasing power into the American economy was more necessary than a balanced budget. Until then he was in danger of repeating domestically his impotence in foreign affairs — of being a preacher without sanctions. He had been denouncing the "economic royalists" who had "owned the Government of the United States from 1921 to 1933." (Some of the 1.8 million who had lost their jobs in the autumn of 1937 might have been quite glad to get back to 1921.) Once he decided in favor of deficit spending, he was in a much stronger position, and by June 1938 he had got a $3.75 billion spending program through without too much difficulty. The trouble was closer to home. Morgenthau threatened to resign on the issue. He was persuaded away from it only by heavy arm-twisting from FDR. Morgenthau, the president is reported to have said, would "go down to history as having quit under fire." Even so, he might have departed had he not been so much of a Roosevelt client.

That Roosevelt chose to have Harry Hopkins with him for the arm-twisting session symbolizes the strength of the position Hopkins occupied for several years from there forward. Hopkins, semirestored after a long period in the hospital, was both the advocate and the agent of deficit finance. "We shall tax and tax, and spend and spend, and elect and elect" was reputed to be his mantra. He was so much a favorite (although never a cloying one) during those dark 1938 days that Roosevelt looked to him as a preferred presidential successor in the 1940 campaign. In fact Hopkins's health, and maybe his personality, although impressive in many ways, were not up to that role. At this stage, with adversity piled on adversity, it is unlikely that Roosevelt's mind embraced the possibility or even the desirability of a third term (against any precedent, but not then forbidden by law) for himself. Indeed the thought was more that he might just decide to curl up and quietly serve out the last two and a half years. His downbeat mood was exacerbated by the wild and wounding rumors about him being circulated and even printed, for his proclaimed welcome of the hatred of the upper classes, in that 1936 speech, had contained more rhetoric than truth.

The rumors ranged from the relatively innocuous view that he had been the most unpopular Harvard undergraduate of the first decade of the twentieth century to the somewhat more up-to-date charge that, apart from being determined to be a dictator, he was clinically insane and probably suffering from syphilis as well. These fantasies were believed by otherwise quite respectable people and led to a considerable confusion in the minds of British and other European observers of the American scene. They looked to Roosevelt as a strong and respected leader who was almost the only beacon of hope in a deteriorating world. Then they discovered that he was the object of hatred verging on contempt in the minds of many of his fellow countrymen whom they were most likely to meet.

Curling up in the face of upper-class rejection was, however, so alien to FDR's spirit and modus operandi that it was hardly a serious danger. Instead, he put his weight behind the last spurt of the New Deal with considerable advances in social security, the minimum wage, and underage employment. On the political front, his activities were less wise, or at least less successful. His irritation with conservative Democratic legislators was wholly understandable. His 1936 victory had brought with it the most Democratic Congress in history. In the Senate, Democrats outnumbered Republicans by 80 to 16, and in the House of Representatives by 343 to 89. When a lot of them joined with the Republicans to block key measures, Roosevelt was affronted. And in what an unfriendly critic described as "a high school girl's revenge," he decided to try to eliminate the worst offenders. He laid down what he thought was a moderate criterion. "Do not misunderstand me," he somewhat defensively began the most significant passage of a speech. "I certainly would not indicate a preference in a State primary merely because a candidate, otherwise liberal in outlook, had consistently differed from me on any single issue. I should be far more concerned about the general attitude of a candidate toward present-day problems and his own inward desire to get practical needs attended to in a practical way."

Moderate or not, this left a vast margin for the subjective judgment of the president. There were undoubtedly some black-hearted reactionaries — particularly, but not exclusively, among the southern senators — and had Roosevelt been able cleanly to eliminate them, it might have been a worthwhile, even an inspiring stage on the journey of the Democratic party toward coherent liberalism. Unfortunately, however, while he (or the recession) succeeded in eliminating many Democrats in the November 1938 midterm elections, they were mostly the wrong ones. And the methods by which he proceeded to this failure were only too supportive of the "high school girl's revenge." He made two sweeps across the country. In the summer, he jogged along (never faster than thirty-five miles an hour) in his private train through Kentucky, Arkansas, Oklahoma, Texas, Colorado, and Nevada to California. He made more than thirty speeches on this swing, and gossip centered on who was allowed to sit next to him, on whom he beamed and on whom he scowled. His first objective was to keep Alben Barkley as senator from Kentucky — Barkley was under heavy challenge from the governor of that state, and his defeat would have meant his replacement as Democratic leader in the Senate by the anathematized Pat Harrison of Mississippi. This was handsomely achieved. Most of the other targets of this swing, however, he missed. In Texas he tried to ostracize Senator Tom Connally, later to be a key figure in the evolution of U.S. foreign policy, but it could be held that he made a better long-term investment by smiling upon the newly elected congressman Lyndon B. Johnson, even though Roosevelt did not live to see it mature. In Nevada, he snubbed without effect Senator Patrick McCarran, and in California he helped the defeat, in spite of Wilsonian affiliations, of Senator McAdoo.

He then went on a two-ocean cruise on U.S.S. *Houston*, through the Panama Canal and up as far as Pensacola, Florida. There he began a southern and still more difficult campaign, winding up, but not in triumph, in Maryland. His triple objective was to defeat three Democratic senators who in all but the historical accident of party label were among the most conservative of legislators. The first was Walter F. George, the mild-mannered but stubbornly uncooperative chairman of the Senate Finance Committee. George represented Georgia, of which Roosevelt, by virtue of his Warm Springs connection, regarded himself as an honorary citizen. The second target was Ellison "Cotton Ed" Smith of South Carolina, whose sobriquet indicated his local strength in the state where the Civil War had begun and who, when someone said that FDR was "his own worst enemy," commented, "Not while I'm alive he's not." And the third was Millard Tydings, of Maryland, who had made the mistake of boasting that he had both "the prestige of Roosevelt and the money of his Republican friends." None of Roosevelt's three enterprises was successful. George, Smith, and Tydings all sailed back into the Senate for another six years.

This was in contrast with the overall election results. By the standard of previous midterms, they were not bad. The Democrats retained a majority in both houses, although their previous preponderance was lopped off. The Republicans gained eighty-one seats in the House; in the Senate, always much slower to move because of the six-year term, they picked up nine. They gained thirteen governorships as well. They were back in the game, if not quite as the Grand Old Party, at least as a major player with hope for a full recovery in 1940.

These were the far from propitious circumstances in which Roosevelt faced the outbreak of the war in Europe in September 1939. Once again the dichotomy between Roosevelt's overseas position as a possible world savior and his relative weakness at home created some confusion. Even such a sophisticated (although also desperately optimistic) observer as Churchill believed in June 1940 that FDR might step in to save France, something of which there was never a realistic chance. Had Roosevelt, like many second-term presidents, subsided toward the close of his second term, looking forward to quiet days at Hyde Park with his stamp collection, how would he have ranked among his predecessors and successors? Somewhere near the top of the second rank is my guess. Perhaps with Andrew Jackson, or Uncle Ted, or Lyndon Johnson: someone who tried hard, who was certainly not negligible, but not unquestionably great either.

The crucial question therefore becomes that of when he embraced the desirability of a third term, thus becoming the president who not only tried imaginatively and semisuccessfully to pull America out of the Great Depression but also led America through its greatest world challenge and, as an almost accidental result of that, saw the problems of low demand and unemployment disappear into the margins.

Had there been a clear successor available, Roosevelt would have found it very difficult to command support for a third term. The Machiavellian theory is therefore that he had carefully built up a number of competing possible successors, all of whom merely had to be exposed to the light of day for it to be obvious how inadequate they were. But this is always a risky course: very few politicians look worthy of the top jobs until they actually come to occupy them. Lord Liverpool, James K. Polk, even Theodore Roosevelt, Harry Truman, and Clement Attlee spring quickly to mind. There is, of course, a much worse pattern, which is that of those who look very well qualified until they actually have to do the job, with Ulysses S. Grant and Anthony Eden as outstanding examples. Also, FDR cannot have been entirely forgetful of the fact that this was the view that Al Smith so mistakenly took of Roosevelt himself when he supported him for governor of New York in 1928.

There were four men mentioned for the Democratic nomination. Roosevelt half promoted Cordell Hull, the venerable secretary of state, and Attorney General Robert H. Jackson. Anti–New Deal Democrats looked to Jack Garner and to James Farley, the New York Catholic politico and servant who aspired to replace his master. They were an unconvincing crew, all of them probably unelectable, even apart from other deficiencies. After their hopes collapsed when Roosevelt was triumphantly drafted at the Democratic convention in July 1940, once again in Chicago as in 1932, they reacted in sharply divergent ways. Hull remained as secretary of state until late 1944, although even less centrally influential than he had been in peacetime. Garner retired sourly to his ranch at Uvalde, Texas, where in spite of, or perhaps because of, his bad temper and his whiskey, he proceeded to live until 1967 and the age of ninety-nine. Farley flounced immediately, bitterly upbraided Roosevelt, retired as postmaster general, and joined the Coca-Cola Company.

Harry Hopkins, over whom Roosevelt's eye had flickered in 1938, was in a different category. He was in his way a first-class man, although prevented by health and maybe, too, by his dependence on Roosevelt's patronage from being a plausible president. In any event, his name had disappeared from contention by 1939. And he became the most enthusiastic organizer of Roosevelt's Chicago draft.

All this leaves unresolved the question of when FDR decided that he wanted to go on being president after January 20, 1941. As late as February 1940 he expressed to Senator Norris of Nebraska, who in spite of a disparity of geography had been one of his strongest supporters in the Tennessee Valley Authority achievement, a genuine argument against running again: "I would have much more trouble with Congress in my third term and much more bitterness to contend with as a result of my running for a third term than I have ever had before." It was a genuine but not necessarily a decisive argument, and should perhaps be interpreted as meaning more that he thought he had come to the end of his New Deal usefulness than that he had ceased to have a further purpose of any sort. He was at the time on the hinge of a famous two-panel cartoon that showed him metamorphosing from "Dr. New Deal" to "Dr. Win the War." And his remarks to Norris should certainly be tempered by a conversation with Morgenthau (whom he knew better than he did Norris) that took place a few weeks earlier. He was then recorded as saying: "I do not want to run again unless between now and the convention things get very very much worse in Europe."

In the next five months a combination of Anglo-French fumbling and Hitler's determination ensured that this condition was satisfied by a more than adequate margin. But there still remains the elusive question of what Roosevelt really wanted for himself. He might think that his stamp collection and a country gentleman's life at Hyde Park (with his mother — still alive until September 1941 — only too welcoming) would be preferable to frustration in Washington. But in his interior being, as one of the great power brokers in the history of the Western world, he probably had a lively awareness of just how bored he would have been.

He also had a clear eye and — more than any of those who closely served him, with the possible exception of Ickes, Morgenthau, and Hopkins — a deeply principled objection to Nazism, as a threat both to civilized values and to the medium-term security of the United States.

So his mind was probably made up by Easter 1940, and his resolve was strengthened by Hitler's subsequent invasion of Norway and Denmark, obliteration of Holland and Belgium, and defeat of France. Roosevelt showed both his growing belligerency and his confidence in the continuation of his presidency by making two nonpartisan Cabinet appointments in June. He retired the two Democratic "peace-horses" at the head of the War and Navy Departments, appointing in their place two strongly internationalist Republicans: Henry L. Stimson, who had been Taft's secretary of war and Hoover's secretary of state, went to the War Department (which contained the army), and Frank Knox, the Chicago publisher who had been Landon's running mate in 1936 (against Roosevelt), went to the Navy Department. FDR was nonetheless determined that if he was to breach for the first time the precedent that George Washington had set in 1796 of not accepting a third term, it had to be done out of reluctant duty, a result of spontaneous demand and not of incontinent campaigning on his own behalf. This he achieved with all the precise political skill that had deserted him for the previous two years but that remained a natural part of his armory. The result of the first and only Chicago ballot was Roosevelt 946, Farley 72, Garner 6, Tydings 9, and Hull 5.

Roosevelt's motives for fighting a third time undoubtedly included his belief that he could do more than any other candidate to help resist the Nazi tide in Europe. But once he had embraced the electoral struggle at home he temporarily but ruthlessly subordinated his European concerns to his determination to win the election. There was an added complication. Until at least early July 1940, Roosevelt had far from full confidence in Britain's will or ability to fight on alone. Nor did he have great trust in Churchill during the latter's first few weeks of premiership in May 1940. He thought Churchill was better than Chamberlain, but that was not saying much. He had, in fact, asked Churchill to write direct to him after his return to the Admiralty in September 1939, something which led to the "Naval Person/Former Naval Person" correspondence, in which about ten letters were exchanged; even so, it may be that Roosevelt had not entirely got over Churchill's alleged snub to him when, as assistant secretary of the navy, he met the future prime minister in London in 1919.

Of more recent impact was the report of Sumner Welles, Cordell Hull's undersecretary of state, whom Roosevelt had sent on a European trip in February–March 1940 to help him make up his mind as to how far his criterion for a third term of "things getting very much worse in Europe" was likely to be met. Welles was a clever man, as sophisticated as Hull was homespun. Nevertheless his tour was, at least seen from a British perspective, as unfortunate as is easily possible to imagine. It stands out in stark and degrading contrast with Harry Hopkins's mission of just under a year later.

Welles went to Paris, Berlin, Rome, and London. He was impressed by Hitler, partly on the irrelevant ground that he spoke a clear, simple German of which Welles could understand every single word (de Gaulle, mutatis mutandis, should have stood at least as high in his regard), and even more by Mussolini. The European statesman of whom he most disapproved was Churchill, whom he thought whiskey-sodden, self-indulgent (he reported a twenty-four-inch cigar, although Churchill's were in fact less than half as long and mostly chewed rather than smoked), and intolerably loquacious. Undoubtedly his report had some influence on Roosevelt, who in April delivered one of his most sententious and, to an Englishman of the period, intolerably patronizing remarks: "The thing that made me hopping mad," FDR told Morgenthau, "is where were the British Fleet when the Germans went up to Bergen and Oslo? It is the most outrageous thing." Maybe it was. The Norwegian campaign was certainly not well handled by the British, and it was one of the most beneficent accidents of history that this mismanagement resulted in Churchill, who was the minister mainly responsible, being swept into the supreme office, from which he had seemed so remote a year or two before. But Roosevelt, still carefully safeguarding his neutrality of action if not of thought, was not the best person to say so.

Roosevelt's respect for Churchill was much strengthened when, after the defeat of France, the British prime minister, probably the most naturally francophile of all twentieth-century British prime ministers (with the possible exception of Anthony Eden), brutally engaged the considerable

French fleet at three points around the North African littoral in early July. Paradoxically, it had the same effect on the American liberal president as on the right-wing Tory backbenchers in the House of Commons, who were naturally Chamberlainite; and for the first time, after Churchill had sunk a few French ships off Oran, Roosevelt felt that he meant business.

This new confidence did not, however, prevent the president from taking on his surprising Republican opponent, Wendell Willkie, who was essentially a liberal internationalist and whose main quarrel with Roosevelt was on the somewhat narrow ground that as president of the Commonwealth and Southern Electric Company he was not enamored of Roosevelt's plan for bringing cheap power to the South. The 1940 campaign, viewed from outside and in retrospect, seems to me one of the more discreditable illustrations in American history of how party politics makes monkeys of so many otherwise fine men. A president who was persuaded to run again by the threat of Hitlerism and a tousled industrialist who was trying to defeat him (and did much better than Hoover in 1932 or Landon in 1936) did battle on the issue, in which neither of them believed, of how America could best keep unentangled from European engagement. Willkie came increasingly to label FDR a warmonger. Roosevelt responded by making the famous Boston speech of October 30, in which he said: "We will not participate in foreign wars and will not need our army, naval or air forces to fight in foreign wars outside of the Americas except in case of attack." Then, in Philadelphia a few days later, he went even further and said: "Your boys are not going to be sent into any foreign wars." Here the "except in case of attack" was omitted. Whether necessary or not — there was some indication that at this stage, with the Blitz raining upon London, American opinion in favor of intervention may have been ahead of the president — his dissimulation worked. On November 5, 1940, Roosevelt beat Willkie by 27 million votes to 22 million, and carried thirty-eight states to give him an electoral college preponderance of 449 to 82. It was not a repeat of 1936 or even of 1932, but it was a solid enough victory for the first man in American history to run for a third time. He had become at once the most popular and the most vilified of the thirty-two presidents to date.

6

Backing into War

Roosevelt's own practical (as opposed to rhetorical) contribution to the Allied cause had been the "destroyers for bases" deal of September 3, 1940. Even this had taken some time to arrange. Churchill, striking a more peremptory note than he normally did with Roosevelt, had written on July 30: "I cannot understand why, with the position as it is, you do not send me 50 or 60 of your oldest destroyers. . . . Mr. President, with great respect, I must tell you that in the long history of the world this is a thing to do now." It was done five weeks later, but the deal was at least as favorable for the Americans as for the British. The United States got long leases on a range of valuable defensive bases from Newfoundland to the West Indies. Britain got the destroyers, but their antiquity was such that by February 1941 only nine of them had been found fit for service even in the desperately pressed British navy.

Nevertheless, Churchill was grateful and

on August 20, before the deal was announceable but when it was well in train, he delivered one of his most memorable passages about Anglo-American relations. He compared them with the flow of a great river: "I could not stop it if I wished; no-one can stop it. Like the Mississippi it just keeps rolling along. Let it roll. Let it roll in full flood, inexorable, irresistible, benignant, to broader lands and better days." He was, of course, engaged in the delicate game of enticing Roosevelt to his side. "Never did any lover woo his mistress more determinedly than I did Franklin Roosevelt," he was to say several years later.* And he did so because he long knew that while Britain could provide a crucial bastion of resistance, it could never win, though it might stave off defeat, without the assistance of the United States.

A week before this Churchill speech, Roosevelt had scraped over an even more

*On the other hand he also said (on his way to Washington after Pearl Harbor in December 1941), "Previously we were trying to seduce them. Now they are secure in the harem." Even the closest relations between states and statesmen are determined by a mixture of sentiment and realpolitik. Neither is necessarily hypocritical.

severe nerve-testing hurdle, although one that made less impact on the outside world and on Britain in particular. On August 13, a six-month extension of the Selective Service Act (which the Senate had endorsed by the reasonably comfortable margin of 50 to 45, although with the Democrats registering well under their full strength) was passed in the House by exactly one vote, 203 to 202. Without it, the United States would have been left without an effective army, and FDR would have been still more of a preacher moralizing from impotence. It would be difficult to exaggerate the impact of this narrowest of narrow shaves upon Roosevelt. It underlined his instinctive view of the dangers of the tightrope that he was walking, and made him impatient of those in his Cabinet, principally Ickes and the new and self-confident Republican recruit Stimson, backed by Knox and Attorney General Robert Jackson, who could not understand his reluctance to be far ahead of public opinion.

To what extent were Roosevelt's views and behavior changed by his liberating second reelection victory? The true answer, I think, is that his views changed hardly at all — he had always been viscerally opposed to Nazism, and therefore committed to its defeat — but his behavior very substantially. Britain, by the time of the American election, was in the trough of the Blitz. This gave it a much more sympathetic position in American eyes than had been the case six months previously. American correspondents, led by the mahogany-voiced Edward R. Murrow and living mostly in a mixture of surrounding luxury and self-induced squalor in the Savoy Hotel, painted a vivid picture of London's defiant vitality. It was much more support-arousing than the days when the Wehrmacht was slicing through France, and a decadent Britain seemed unlikely to withstand the Germans much better.

There were several indications that Roosevelt was cautiously following rather than leading American opinion. He did, however, make two crucial decisions in December 1940, both of which were to some extent responses to a letter that Churchill sent to him on December 8, after many drafts. This has been described by James MacGregor Burns, with maybe a touch of hyperbole, as "perhaps the most important letter of his [Churchill's] life." Although there were a few subsidiary points, it was essentially an appeal for greater American assistance (although not, Churchill assured the president, "a large American expeditionary army") in the battle of the North Atlantic, the effective sundering of which link was Britain's most immediate current threat, and a plea that his country not be "stripped to the bone" in an attempt to pay cash for every item of equipment provided by the Americans. "If, as I believe you are convinced, Mr. President," Churchill robustly ended, "that the defeat of the Nazi and Fascist tyranny is a matter of high consequence to the people of the United States and to the Western Hemisphere, you will regard this letter not as an appeal for aid, but as a statement of the minimum action necessary to achieve our common purpose."

The president received the communication when on a ten-day Caribbean cruise, accompanied, apart from his immediate staff, only by Harry Hopkins. It aroused no immediate reaction. Then, a couple of evenings later, according to Hopkins, "he suddenly came out with it — the whole program." Thus was Lend-Lease born.

There followed an intensive and exceptionally decisive two weeks back in Washington. The result was presented to the nation and the world in a press conference on December 17. It was a striking example both of Roosevelt's self-confidence and of his liking for a somewhat rambling informality that he chose this medium for many of his most important pronouncements. Churchill would have regarded press conferences as insufficiently resonant sounding boards and might also (falsely) have been hesitant about his ability to put his most important words into an only semiprepared context. "Now what I am trying to do," Roosevelt began the central passage, with what might have been thought to be doubtful persuasiveness, "is to eliminate the dollar sign . . . get rid of the silly, foolish old dollar sign." Then he continued with one of the most famous similes of the twentieth century.

Well, let me give you an illustration: Suppose my neighbor's home catches fire, and I have a length of garden hose four or five hundred feet away. If I can take my garden hose and connect it up with his hydrant, I may help him to put out his fire. Now, what do I do? I don't say to him before that operation, "Neighbor, my garden hose cost me $15; you will have to pay me $15 for it." What is the transaction that goes on? I don't want $15 — I want my garden hose back after the fire is over. All right. If it goes through the fire all right, intact, without any damage to it, he gives it back to me and thanks me very much for the use of it. But suppose it gets smashed up — holes in it — during the fire; we don't have to have too much formality about it. . . . He says, "All right, I will replace it." Now, if I get a nice garden hose back, I am in pretty good shape.

The simile was as brilliantly homespun as it was misleading. How on earth he thought the British were going to return intact tanks and destroyers after the war, much less replace them if they were smashed up, or what use this equipment would be to America if it *were* returned was not remotely clear. However, the speech worked, received a favorable response from the American public, and had the great advantage that, unlike several of Roosevelt's pronouncements in this twilight between peace and war, its two steps forward were not weakened by at least one step back at a subsequent press conference. Perhaps that was the great advantage of starting with a press conference rather than a highfalutin speech, from which he only too frequently proceeded to remove the sting when he met the press the following day.

This time the follow-up took the form of a Fireside Chat on the evening of December 29, when, if anything, he strengthened his message. "The experience of the past two years," Roosevelt said, "has proven beyond doubt that no nation can appease the Nazis. No man can turn a tiger into a kitten by stroking it." The only note of reservation was this: "Our national policy is not directed toward war. Its sole purpose is to keep war away from our country and our people." But he quickly added, "We must be the great arsenal of democracy."

His second crucial decision of the period was to send Harry Hopkins on a mission to England in January 1941. Hopkins arrived by flying boat on January 9, was met by Brendan Bracken, Churchill's man Friday, at Poole harbor on the Dorset coast, and was taken to London, where Churchill gave him a luncheon *à deux,* which lasted until four o'clock. Then he took him for the weekend to Ditchley Park in north Oxfordshire, which was thought to be safer than Chequers on nights of a high moon, and exposed him to some of his most rakish friends. Thereafter, in the course of this first visit, which extended itself to just over a month, twice its expected length, Hopkins spent eleven evenings dining with Churchill, spent three weekends at Chequers as well as making another visit to Ditchley, and was taken both to look at enemy-occupied coast from Dover and to Scotland, first to the fleet at Scapa Flow and then to see Churchill dealing with the Labour city council in Glasgow, at once the center of "Red Clydeside" and a vital shipbuilding and munitions center.

It was the full treatment, and it worked brilliantly, but the effect was also based upon a real if surprising affinity between Churchill and Hopkins. Essentially, this stemmed from the fact that Hopkins, a poor boy from Sioux City become a welfare worker in the 1920s and 1930s, was, like many of those whose company Churchill most enjoyed, a sophisticated outsider with a touch of loucheness. He had a mordant humor, he liked gambling at racetracks, and he was easily at home in any company where the tone was not too pious. At first the affinity was determined on Churchill's part, arising from the extreme view, expressed by Bracken but probably inspired by Churchill, that Hopkins "was the most important visitor to this country he had ever had." But it then became spontaneous; in my considered judgment, Churchill and Hopkins were closer, in the sense that they were more at ease in each other's company, than Churchill and Roosevelt ever were. The two great superstars of the twentieth century, the twin-headed Western leadership that won World War II (even if it needed crucial assistance from Stalin), basically required their own unimpeded orbits, although they could quite enjoy each other's company for limited periods.[*] Hopkins was an essential link between them, but Churchill was more in tune with the link than he was with the principal.

Hopkins's most committing statement had been made at a relatively intimate Glasgow dinner (perhaps thirty people) on January 15. Impressed a little by the activities of the day, and maybe by the quality of

[*]Exactly captured by Churchill's remark at a Marrakech dinner on January 1, 1944, to his naval aide Commander Thompson: "But, Tommy, you will bear witness to the fact that I do not repeat my stories so often as does my dear friend, the President of the United States."

the hospitality, he had quoted the Book of Ruth on the future of Anglo-American relations: "Wither thou goest I will go; and where thou lodgest, I will lodge: thy people shall be my people and thy God my God." "Even to the end," Hopkins added. Churchill was in tears, never too difficult a result to achieve, but on this occasion justifiably so. It was for him almost as decisive a moment as when he received the news of Pearl Harbor, and of America's enforced entry into the war.

Nevertheless, in the still fairly desperate circumstances of early 1941, Britain could not survive on the Book of Ruth, and Roosevelt had to provide some backup for Hopkins's emotion. This he fulfilled by getting the Lend-Lease bill through the House by the relatively comfortable majority of 260 to 160 in mid-February, and through the Senate in mid-March. Also, and perhaps of more imminent significance, the United States moved to take over responsibility for the western half of the Atlantic. On April 9, America acquired the right to establish bases in Greenland, and two days later Roosevelt announced that he was extending the area that the U.S. Navy would patrol to midway between the westernmost bulge of Africa and the easternmost bulge of Brazil. This was an immediate and predicable response to Britain's greatest vulnerability of the time, which was the effective severance of the North Atlantic link by U-boat action. Lend-Lease was not going to be much good if the matériel, however paid for, could not arrive except at the price of unacceptable losses at sea. It also meant that Churchill could comfort himself for such losses as occurred with the thought that they contributed to his desideratum of U.S. entry into the war. And, indeed, such engagements as occurred in the eight months between then and Pearl Harbor, despite Hitler's general desire not to provoke America, came near to belligerency. Had Japan not existed it is difficult to decide how long it would have taken for the cautious Roosevelt, despite his bellicosity of 1914–17, to have followed Woodrow Wilson into an Atlantic-provoked war. His commitment to defend the shipping lanes was increased by his July 1940 decision to take over the garrisoning of Iceland from the British. As this shows, he was anxious to help Britain, but he was wary of getting ahead of congressional and public opinion.

These American steps to some extent compensated for the setbacks that continued in Europe. In early April 1941, the

Germans attacked Yugoslavia and Greece. Within a week they were in Belgrade. Greece took another two weeks, but when it, too, was forced to surrender there were 55,000 British troops in the country, ill-spared from Egypt, many of whom were lost. The Greeks and the British fell back on the island of Crete, against which the Germans performed a brilliant airborne operation. Crete held out until early June but the forced evacuation, immortalized in the *Officers and Gentlemen* volume of Evelyn Waugh's war trilogy, provided a further British humiliation. The savage joke was that there was only one military activity at which the British were superior to the Germans. This was evacuations, because the British had so much more practice. Except around Britain itself, the Germans were still manifestly winning the war.

Nevertheless, Roosevelt continued with the policy of hoping that events would push America in a more interventionist direction. At an April 25 Cabinet meeting, he told the malcontents that the extension of the U.S. Atlantic patrolling zone was "a step forward." Stimson responded, "Well, I hope you will keep on walking, Mr. President. Keep on walking," a sally that was greeted by a mixture of laughter and approval around the table. Several members said that they had never before heard the president spoken to like that in his Cabinet. Normally, whether in a Cabinet meeting or at a press conference, he made the jokes, and the audience laughed sycophantically. That this time it was the other way around perhaps illustrated the disadvantages of appointing a Republican who was well senior to himself and had nothing to lose, being more sought after than seeking: always a crucially strong position for a nominal subordinate.

Some thought that Roosevelt in the early summer of 1941 was a president in search of an incident, which Hitler had the sense to try to avoid providing. Perhaps Roosevelt's most significant contribution during June was not to make difficulties when Hitler launched Operation Barbarossa against Russia, and Churchill wanted to provide help for the Soviet Union. The latter's most characteristic aphorism on that issue was when he said (privately): "If Hitler invaded Hell I would at least make a favourable reference to the Devil." The paradox was that Churchill had a far more intense (almost obsessive) anti-Communist record than did Roosevelt, but that Roosevelt presided over a country with more anti-Communist neurosis than Britain, and was also more sensitive to the gusts of public opinion than was Churchill. The immediate consequence of Roosevelt's enthusiastic agreement was that he and Churchill did not get out of step about providing aid to Russia. Therefore, when, within twenty-four hours of the German invasion, Churchill made the broadcast of which the key sentence was "Any man or state who fights against Nazism will have our aid," he was not taking a risk with respect to the White House.

So the response to Hitler's invasion of Russia never came near to producing an Anglo-American rupture. Indeed Roosevelt and Churchill were bound together, if not exactly with hoops of steel at least in the dismal conviction that the Red Army could hold out against the full force of the Wehrmacht for only a few months, but that in their joint interest it was desirable to extend this period as long as possible.

Meanwhile, preparations went ahead for Hopkins's scheme of a meeting between his old (but not fading) hero, Roosevelt, and his new hero, Churchill. Curiosity on both sides strengthened the joint impulse. The meeting, a very naval occasion, took place in Placentia Bay, Newfoundland, in mid-August 1941. The president arrived in a U.S. cruiser to which he had surreptitiously transferred from the presidential yacht off Martha's Vineyard. Churchill, from a smaller country, needed a bigger ship, but with the good excuse that he came across the Atlantic and not just up the eastern coast of America. On the first day (a Saturday) Churchill went to greet Roosevelt on the *Augusta*, the American ship. On meeting him, the prime minister handed over a letter, almost of introduction, from King George VI, who by a curious quirk, and because his 1939 American state visit had included a Hyde Park weekend, at that stage knew Roosevelt much better than did Churchill. Roosevelt received the letter and its bearer with the encouraging remark that "at last we've gotten together."

On that first day Churchill had both main meals on the *Augusta*, the first alone with Roosevelt and Hopkins, the second with a full complement of high officers from both countries.* After this, Churchill was invited to give his appreciation of the

---

*It is intriguing to speculate whether the U.S. Navy dry rule was temporarily lifted in response to the eminence of the guests and their tastes. Otherwise Churchill must have had a fairly miserable day, particularly when he was asked to perform (on Coca-Cola?) after dinner.

war and offered a pungent *tour d'horizon.* The next day Roosevelt came to the British ship, where a "church militant" service was held under the big guns. The choice of hymns was suited to the occasion: "For Those in Peril on the Sea" (better known in America as "Eternal Father, Strong to Save"), "Onward, Christian Soldiers," and "O God, Our Help in Ages Past." The whole ship's company joined in the singing, and both Roosevelt and Churchill were appropriately moved. The occasion, and particularly the first hymn, were subsequently given a special poignancy by the fate of the British men and officers. Many of them were drowned when the grand battleship was sunk by the Japanese off Malaya four months later.

After the service, there was a British lunch, which was certainly not dry, and then two days of conference before the ships sailed off in different directions on the Tuesday afternoon. In some ways, the most valuable part of the encounter was the establishment of relations between the service chiefs of the two countries, which became of increasing importance in 1942, 1943, and 1944. The two principals also broke a good deal of ice. Their joint communiqué, which subsequently became known as the Atlantic Charter, attracted a lot of attention, but it was perhaps the meeting's least important outcome. It certainly did not commit Roosevelt to war, or even to a tough warning line against the Japanese, which the British wanted. Most of it was taken up with a fairly misty eight-point statement of postwar aims; this did no harm, but Churchill instinctively thought that beating Hitler was a sufficient war aim, and Roosevelt could be accused of putting the cart before the horse by proclaiming the aims of a war that he was still reluctant to enter. Actually FDR had already voiced war aims when he set forth the Four Freedoms in his January State of the Union message: freedom of speech and expression, freedom of worship, freedom from want, freedom from fear.

Back in Washington, Roosevelt prepared one of his familiar "two steps forward, one step back" dances. Asked about the significance of the Newfoundland meeting he said: "Exchange of views. That's all. Nothing else." Asked whether it meant the United States was any closer to entering the war, he said: "I should say, no." The debate between isolationists and interventionists was growing every day more savage. Charles A. Lindbergh, once a national hero, declared that "the three most important groups who have been pressing this country toward war are the British, the Jewish, and the Roosevelt administration."

Roosevelt's general attitude on the Jewish question was a little confused. He had many Jewish advisers, and desperate opponents denounced his "Jew Deal." But immigration laws limited the entry of refugees from Hitler's pogroms, and the genteel anti-Semitism of the day influenced the State Department, especially through FDR's friend from the Wilson administration Breckinridge Long, now in charge of visas for refugees. But in the end, as Professor Gerhard L. Weinberg reminds us, the United States "accepted about twice as many Jewish refugees as the rest of the world put together: about 200,000 out of 300,000."

Putting one Spanish dance upon another, Roosevelt then supplemented the Catalan *sardana*, with its rather boring steps backward and forward, with a much more complicated fandango with the Japanese. Here the complications were almost infinite. Cordell Hull worked for a settlement, sometimes assisted by Emperor Hirohito, although rather weakly for such a godlike as well as imperial figure, together with his prime minister, Prince Fumimaro Konoe, and the two Japanese ambassadors then in Washington, one regular, one special. On the other hand, the American ambassador in Tokyo, Joseph C. Grew, a Grotonian like Roosevelt, provided a striking example of an ambassador who had not gone native and favored a hard line. So did Stimson, Ickes, and Knox. In Japan, most of the military chiefs were equally recalcitrant. In October Prime Minister Konoe resigned, exhausted by the rigors of the dance, and was replaced by the more aggressive Tojo. Even so, Cordell Hull kept a dialogue going (he was said to have spent at least a hundred hours talking to the Japanese ambassador Kichisaburo Nomura at the State Department), and his persistence in seeking conciliation was fully in accordance with Roosevelt's own views. Roosevelt was cautious for one bad and one good reason. The bad one was his frequent natural hesitancy. The good one was that he was fairly determined on an Atlantic strategy of "Germany first" if it came to war. It would have been easy for him, as a follower of American opinion, to have preferred a Pacific priority. Britain was very lucky that Roosevelt's instinctive preference was all the other way. He was even eager to transfer part of the Pacific fleet from Hawaii to the Atlantic.

When he sanctioned an oil embargo against the Japanese to demonstrate opposition to their war in China and their occupation of French Indochina, Roosevelt had no intention of driving them precipitously to war with the United States. It was Ickes who dictated the draconian terms of the embargo. When confronted by that fait accompli, Roosevelt forbore to reverse it; this may indeed have been a major factor leading Tokyo toward war.

Nevertheless, Hull's negotiations with the Japanese ambassadors continued at their urging. So when Pearl Harbor was attacked with no prior notice, the sense of betrayal that embraced both Hull and the president was wholly understandable. When Nomura came to the State Department to declare war at two p.m. (Washington time) on Sunday, December 7 (an hour after the attack), Hull replied with affronted southern dignity: "In all my fifty years of public service I have never seen a document that was more crowded with infamous falsehoods and distortions — infamous falsehoods and distortions on a scale so huge that I never imagined until today that any government on the planet was capable of uttering them." Roosevelt, always a greater master of the succinct and memorable phrase, referred to December 7 in his address to Congress on the following day as "a date which will live in infamy." In this speech he asked for a declaration of war (hardly an issue) on Japan, but not on Germany or Italy. This was left for Hitler, conveniently but unwisely it may be thought, to do a few days later. Italy obediently followed.

To what extent did things fall out as Roosevelt wanted? The extreme view is that Roosevelt (through Magic, the Japanese cipher, which the Americans were already reading) was given advance warning of the attack on Pearl Harbor, but chose to ignore it in order to ensure American entry into the war. This is manifest nonsense. The idea that he, the most navy-loving of all presidents of the United States, would have left eight battleships at their moorings in order to be destroyed or greatly damaged by the Japanese is absurd. Furthermore, he would have needed compliance in the plot from Stimson and Knox, as well as from General George Marshall and Admiral Harold Stark. Nor was anything to be gained by allowing the great ships to be destroyed at their moorings if they could have been alerted and at sea. An ineffective Japanese attack would have been just as good a casus belli — assuming that one was sought — as the deadly one, which, together with British naval defeats around Singapore, temporarily put every ocean of the world, except for the Atlantic, under Japanese superiority.

Then there is the view that it was the British who were behind the whole plot. Of course Churchill desperately wanted America in the war. When he heard the news of Pearl Harbor he said, with spontaneous frankness, "So we have won after all." Whether the old imperialist would have chosen for America's entry to come as it did is a different matter. Pearl Harbor's auxiliary events led to the greatest defeats the British empire had ever experienced: two great battleships, *Prince of Wales* and *Repulse*, at the bottom of the sea; Malaya, Singapore, and, soon afterward, Hong Kong occupied by the new enemy. These setbacks led to one of the lowest moments of Churchill's wartime premiership, in early 1942.

Furthermore, subordinate only to Churchill's desire to see America in the war was his wish that, once in, they should give priority to an Atlantic rather than a Pacific strategy. On his voyage to Chesapeake Bay in another battleship, starting less than a week later, he spent most of his working time cogitating how he would persuade the president. When he got to the White House he discovered, to his surprise and delight, that he was pushing at an open door. But engineering (even if he could) the devastating attack on Pearl Harbor would hardly have been the most obvious method of effecting this.

So both Roosevelt and Churchill can be fairly acquitted of having plotted Pearl Harbor. There is the separate point of whether either or both of them were, in the autumn of 1941, hoping for some incident, preferably in the Atlantic, that would bring America into the war. The answer in Churchill's case is certainly yes. In Roosevelt's case, it is much more equivocal. During the summer of 1941 he both said to Ickes that he "was not willing to fire the first shot," and informed Morgenthau, "I am waiting to be pushed into the situation." James MacGregor Burns thought that if ever there was a point when he knowingly crossed the threshold between aiding Britain in order to stay out of the war and aiding Britain in order to join in the war, July 1941 was probably the time. On the other hand, Harry Hopkins recorded that when he lunched with Roosevelt as the Pearl Harbor news began to come in on December 7, the president

> discussed at some length his efforts to keep the country out of the war and his earnest desire to complete his administration without war, so that if this action of Japan's were true it would take the matter entirely out of his hands, because the Japanese have made the decision for him.

Hopkins did not record with memorable succinctness, but he did try to record the truth. And this would have been a moment, and Hopkins a companion, at which and to whom even Roosevelt might have been expected to reveal his innermost thoughts. Nevertheless the verdict must be this: Roosevelt approached war with his habitual ambiguity. But once the decision had been taken for him, there was no ambiguity about his determination to be the president who won the greatest war in American history.

7

The Hard-Fought Years:
December 1941–July 1944

Although in retrospect it looks improbable, when the United States was in the war and the Russian front had held for six months, the Allied victory was not a foregone conclusion. The adage that "we must never forget that there was a time when events now in the past were still in the future" has considerable relevance here. If the Germans had got the atom bomb first, or if they had smashed their way through to the Caucasus instead of being held at Stalingrad; if the North Atlantic link had been further attenuated; if the pressure (mainly Russian but to some extent American, too) for a premature second front in France had led to a hurling back into the sea, with terrible casualties, of a premature Anglo-American assault; if, even, the last wave of aerial bombardment of Britain, with the sinister V-1s and V-2s, had had a longer run against a war-weary people, the victory might in one case (the A-bomb) have gone the other way, or in the others been delayed for nearly half a decade.

How much did Roosevelt contribute to the containment of these hazards and to the successful outcome? First, his fame and his personality almost effortlessly made him the accepted captain of the Allies. At the beginning of 1942, Churchill came back to Washington from a short Ottawa interlude for the setting up of the United Nations (a name that has since become misleading, because of confusion with the post-1945 international organization) as the overarching body for inter-Allied cooperation in the war. There was no argument about the United States being the first signatory, or about Britain being the second, but the original proposal that the former British dominions should come next, with the European governments in exile in London or Cairo following, and with China and Russia bringing up the rear, quickly foundered. China and Russia were brought up to the third and fourth places. But the significant fact was that no one even suggested that the United States, the most recent recruit, should be other than number one. It could be weakly argued that this was because Roosevelt was the only head of government among the Allies who was also head of state. On a formal level this would have been equally true fifty years earlier, but no one then ever dreamed of suggesting that at an international gathering or grouping President Benjamin Harrison should have been given a leadership role over Lord Salisbury, the contemporary British prime minister. The imperial presidency effectively began at that White House signing ceremony on January 1, 1942, and Franklin Roosevelt's personality and world fame assisted its easy birth. I doubt that Churchill, still less Stalin, would equally freely have ceded the prime spot to Willkie, let alone Stimson or Farley, had one of them triumphed in 1940.

Roosevelt's style of leadership at home was much quieter than that of Churchill, more relaxed it might be said, and of course immensely less authoritarian than that of Stalin. At the first effective engagement of the top political and military members of the two countries — the Washington Arcadia Conference of December 1941–January 1942 — there was surprise on the American side at the constant bustle on the British side, with secretaries hurrying in and out carrying the heavy red dispatch boxes with which British ministers, now to the mild bemusement of their European Union counterparts, try to impress the world with the historic symbols of great imperial responsibilities that they continue to employ. The British, per contra, were struck by the air of relative calm that pervaded and by how Roosevelt operated in a much more isolated way than did Churchill. They sensibly attributed this not to lethargy but to the secure exercise of power. The sometimes admiring but more often critical diaries of Field Marshal Lord Alanbrooke, chief of the Imperial General Staff from 1941 to 1946, reveal him incarcerated in postmidnight meetings with Churchill on several evenings a week, as well as being bombarded with minutes from the prime minister. Roosevelt rarely saw General Marshall more than a couple of times a month, never at night, and left him almost free of minutes save for occasional formal approvals. In fact, both military heads nearly always got their way with their political masters, although Alanbrooke was made to argue his case far more strenuously.

Yet Roosevelt never let grand strategy go out of his hands, and as the war went on he also became the increasingly powerful partner in the west. At first Churchill, in substance if not in form, trailing clouds of resistant glory and with Roosevelt "securely in the harem," could almost claim a mildly superior or at least an equal position. This was true at the Arcadia Conference, and was maybe still the case at the beginning of Churchill's June 1942 Hyde Park and Washington visit. But when, midway through that visit, the 35,000-man British garrison in Tobruk surrendered, thereby annulling General Wavell's 1941 victories in the Western Desert of Egypt and Libya and creating a great need in Churchill for American psychological sustenance, it was the beginning of the end of that phase. By the Casablanca Conference of January 1943, the United States was becoming the preponderant Western partner. This is so even though General Marshall and War Secretary Stimson thought they had been outwitted into following the British Mediterranean strategy rather than imposing their own strong preference for hitting the enemy on his snout at the Western Wall in France. However, it was Roosevelt who acted as the principal matchmaker in bringing together, in a loveless temporary marriage, the French generals de Gaulle and Giraud. Giraud — much more than Field Marshal Haig, the British commander in France in World War I, to whom the phrase was first applied — was a man who was "brilliant to the tops of his boots"; he was quickly eaten up by his putative partner de Gaulle. With rather more permanent impact, Roosevelt was also allowed to carry Churchill along with him in his sudden proclamation of the doctrine of unconditional surrender, which, according to Eisenhower's dubious estimate, prolonged the war by between sixty and ninety days.

This American preponderance was more evident at the conference code-named Trident in Washington in May 1943, when Roosevelt himself, much though he disliked confrontation, directly challenged Churchill's peripheral strategy aimed at Italy and the Balkans. And it was still more plain at the two Quebec Conferences, of August 1943 and September 1944. It was even the case at the two Tripartite Conferences with Stalin, the first at Teheran in November 1943 and the second at Yalta in January 1945. By Teheran, still more by Yalta, the Russians had turned themselves from surly suppliants for Anglo-American aid (as they had been in 1941) into the dominant military power in Europe. The Battle of Stalingrad in the autumn of 1942 more or less coincided with the Battle of El Alamein, which removed the threat to

many with a flick of his coattails. In Nebraska, he strongly supported Senator George Norris, who was defeated. And in New York, in his own Dutchess County, he tried hard, with a good deal of outward-looking Republican support, to get rid of Congressman Hamilton Fish, who together with Barton and Martin had constructed his trio of obloquy in the 1940 campaign. Fish survived triumphantly. FDR had also, in parliamentary terms, got himself "paired" with Wendell Willkie, whom he had encouraged to go on a world tour, so that both parties had to campaign in 1942 in the absence of the men who had led them two years previously. The 1942 midterm elections were also notable for the emergence of Thomas E. Dewey, who was elected governor of New York State by the convincing plurality of 600,000, the first Republican to be so since 1920. But in fact the election paved the way to Dewey's being, with William Jennings Bryan and Adlai Stevenson, one of the three great presidential also-rans of the twentieth century. He lost to Roosevelt in 1944 and to Truman in 1948.

Throughout the second half of 1941 and 1942, Roosevelt had remained essentially dissatisfied with the progress of American industrial mobilization. Output was increasing, but too slowly to meet America's manifold commitments: to equip its own forces, to keep up Lend-Lease supplies to Britain, and, from midsummer on, to meet at any rate some part of the insatiable demands of Stalin. In the last case there was considerable doubt in American public opinion as to whether it ought to be done at all. The isolationists, recognizing that they faced defeat on the issue of aid to Britain, dug in on a new line of anti-Communist defense.

The *Chicago Tribune*, ex-president Hoover, and Senator Robert A. Taft of Ohio, then emerging to national prominence, constituted a trio of resistance. Taft said that a Communist victory would be far more dangerous than a Fascist one (not a very likely prospect in the summer of 1941; many others opposed aid to Russia on the precisely opposite ground that it would be throwing good matériel after bad — or, at any rate, inadequate — supplies). And even a man of such good common sense as Senator Harry Truman came out with the extraordinary doctrine that if Germany were winning the United States should help Russia, but if Russia were winning maybe the reverse should be done. He did, however, add that the last thing he wanted to see was a Nazi victory. At first this sounds like a remarkably stupid judgment from a man who was subsequently to show such courageous wisdom, but it could, I suppose, be argued that he was in fact demonstrating great prescience and looking ahead to the Berlin airlift of 1948.

Throughout these alarums and excursions Roosevelt kept his head very well. He stuck to his major strategic judgments: that Germany had to be beaten before Japan, and that even before America was in the war this meant that the sustenance of Russia was more important than pandering to anti-Communist feeling. To some extent, he took his cue on this issue from Churchill, who had more historical baggage to dispose of, having been the leading advocate of the early suppression of the Russian Revolution, whereas Roosevelt had (in November 1933) been the first American president to give diplomatic recognition to the Soviet government. But the policy of aid to Russia was also a spontaneous choice of Roosevelt's both before and after Pearl Harbor. Then he fairly quickly formed the view that he could get on better with Stalin than could Churchill, although they never met until the Teheran Conference of October 1943. There was nonetheless something in his proposition. From the time of Hopkins's visit to Moscow in August 1941 there were indications, disturbing for Churchill, that one large landmass might understand another better than the Russians could comprehend a small island that thought its 1940 wound stripes entitled it to more continuing consideration than it received. Roosevelt's occasional suggestions that, since he knew better how to get on with Stalin, it might serve the Allied cause if he had a bilateral meeting with him never failed as a tease of Churchill, even though he himself had two bilateral meetings with Stalin and no fewer than six with Roosevelt. In the event, Churchill managed to frustrate any exclusive Soviet-American get-together, but he became very agitated when Roosevelt, both at Teheran and at Yalta, tried to show himself equidistant between the other two.

Roosevelt's calmness of strategic judgment (perhaps assisted by his knowing less than Churchill about military matters) showed itself in the persistence of his "Germany first" policy, even when Stimson and Marshall were dismayed by his surrendering too easily to Churchill's peripheralism and Mediterranean strategy. The Pentagon urged him at least to threaten to play the "Japan first" card, which would also have been in accord with much of American public opinion. But Roosevelt never weakened on this point, even though at the Trident conference in May 1943 he felt it necessary to speak with unusual directness to Churchill — and in semipublic, too: that is, in the presence of both countries' chiefs of staff — about the latter's desire to be whooshing off on Balkan campaigns, in particular his near obsession with bringing Turkey into the war on the Allied side.

On the home front, Roosevelt's record was more mixed. He dealt harshly with the ethnic Japanese on the West Coast, both those who were still subjects of the emperor and those who were native-born Americans, disrupting their lives by moving them to internment camps and directing his attorney general Francis Biddle to suppress his liberalism. He refused to get involved in black segregationist disputes with the army, thinking that he had enough on his hands, and believing that the appointment of three black colonels by late 1942 ought to be an adequate assuagement. And he allowed his favorite service, the U.S. Navy, to remain almost completely white. He was a good deal better at securing adequate opportunities for blacks (even that involved much thought) in defense plants through the Fair Employment Practices Commission. What he would have thought of the career of General Colin Powell, both as chief of staff and as secretary of state, is easy to appraise. Certainly he would have approved, although he might have explained that he could not be too much in advance of public opinion, which was different in 2001 than it had been in 1942.

On the general defense effort, he was more inclined to appoint temporary "czars" outside the peacetime machinery of government, with overlapping rather than clearly defined individual responsibilities. An exception may have been the Office of Price Administration under Leon Henderson, a tough-minded and committed New Dealer who, assisted by the towering support of John Kenneth Galbraith in his first government job, endeavored to hold down the cost of living. The Office of Production Management was jointly headed by William S. Knudsen, an immigrant who had risen through the assembly line of General Motors to become its manufacturing genius, and Sidney Hillman, the son of immigrants, as a twin-headed eagle. At a press conference, Roosevelt refused to say who was in charge and pretended that two could operate as one. This complacent doctrine foundered, and Hillman went back to his Amalgamated Clothing Workers, one of the prominent New York unions remarkably run by immigrants or their first descendants. The OPM was later superseded by a War Production Board, and James F. Byrnes was persuaded to leave the Supreme Court and join the White House staff as director of war mobilization in a relationship with the president that was personal, exceptional, and transient. Fiorello La Guardia, the mayor of New York, was appointed head of the Office of Civilian Defense, in which he was more of a propagandist than an administrator, but as America never needed much civilian defense this did not matter unduly.

Besides reshuffling these organizations, Roosevelt took seriously the strictures of Harry S Truman's Senate Select Committee to Investigate the National Defense Program on the inadequacies of the defense effort. They were often well founded, and Roosevelt did not regard them as mischievous, as he did the Dies Committee on Un-American Activities, a House committee, named after its chairman, an anti-Roosevelt Democratic congressman from

Texas who paved the way for Senator Joseph McCarthy. Roosevelt thought cooperation with the Truman Committee might be the best way he could show attentiveness to Congress and he proved right, for although the committee made many trenchant criticisms, it also made Truman's reputation as a national politician, and did so without making him unacceptable to the president as a running mate for the 1944 election. Compared with any of the other possible choices — Wallace, Byrnes, Barkley, even Justice William O. Douglas — the selection of Truman was of considerable benefit to the Western world.

The verdict on Roosevelt as leading the transformation of the United States into the "arsenal of democracy" must be distinctly positive. He encountered much business resistance to the conversion to war production, and the Truman Committee exposed much waste and fraud. But in due course the industrial war machine rose magnificently to the challenge. The machine was so powerful by comparison with that of other countries that, if it was given its head and pointed firmly in the right direction, its capacity was immense. And because of the resources of manpower (and womanpower) as well as of production capacity that remained unused after eight and a half years of the New Deal, it could all be done while building up large armed forces — not as great as the Russian, but much greater than the British — and was compatible with rising living standards for much of the population, while limiting inflation. But, as stated earlier, it was perhaps the "monarchical" aspects of encouraging war production that FDR handled best. A classic example of this was provided by his late September trip in 1942. He was away from Washington for two weeks and traveled 8,754 miles (at never more than thirty-five miles an hour) in his beloved special train. He went to Detroit and inspected the Chrysler tank assembly plant, and then to the Ford plant at Willow Run, where, attended by both Henry and Edsel Ford, he saw that half-mile-long assembly line, which had been converted from motors to aircraft. He then went, via Minneapolis and a lake in northern Idaho large enough to serve as a naval training station, to the Pacific Coast, visiting the Boeing plant at Seattle, the Douglas plant at Long Beach, and Henry Kaiser's famous Portland (Oregon) yards, where he watched the launch of a ship of which the keel had been laid only ten days before.

In true princely style, he combined his

official visits with calls upon his scattered family and former satraps: his daughter, Anna, and her husband in Seattle; in Texas, his daughter-in-law Faye, the wife of Elliott Roosevelt (Colonel Elliott — "I'd like to be a colonel, too, darling" in a satirical jingle of the time — was already away at the war); and John Nance Garner, his former vice president with whom, all passion almost spent, he had a friendly reunion, each complimenting the other on how well he looked. It was not so much that Roosevelt looked well — eighteen months later, his doctors were shocked by his high blood pressure and cardiac deterioration — as that he spread an atmosphere of confidence. The jaunty angle of his cigarette holder and the upward tilt of his jaw were worth as much to American morale as were Churchill's chewed cigars and growling phrases to Britain, even though America never had to face the likelihood of defeat that Britain did in 1940. There was, however, also a touch of royalty about Roosevelt's contribution to morale. Although a staunch republican who always addressed crowned heads as though they were, in an appropriate oxymoron, slightly inferior equals, he nonetheless showed exceptional consideration to old Queen

Wilhelmina of the Netherlands and her daughter, Princess (later Queen) Juliana, with both of whom any question of sexual electricity was most unlikely. But his real favorite was Crown Princess Martha of Norway, of whom this could not be said with equal certainty. His correspondence secretary, William Hassett, a craggy Vermonter, expressed some surprise at the amount of time Roosevelt was prepared to devote to such (in his view) frivolous encounters. The seriousness of FDR's attachment to Princess Martha should be tempered by the knowledge that, in the early months of 1942, he had, after a gap of twenty years, begun seeing and going for country drives with Lucy Rutherfurd (Mercer), whose sedate but benevolent husband had suffered a stroke in 1941 that made an invalid of him. (He would die in 1944.) It might, however, be a mistake to assume that Roosevelt, who could keep so many political balls in the air at one time, would have found two ladies (plus a wife) an impossible challenge.

At least after the tripartite Teheran Conference in October 1943, the opening of a second front in France was a settled matter. The commitment to a strengthened Stalin was inevitable; Churchill could not have attempted to delay further without a total break with the Americans, which he could not contemplate. Nevertheless, I regard Churchill's policy of postponing a landing in France until it could be undertaken with a strong possibility of success as one of his greatest wartime services, second only to his frustrating, with great difficulty, any Halifax-Chamberlain attempt to sue for peace in the desperate days of late May 1940. Had the second front been prematurely launched, certainly in 1942, probably in 1943, the result might easily have been abject, with the hurling back into the sea of the Anglo-American forces, appalling casualties, and victory postponed until the late 1940s or even 1950.

This bone of contention with the British having been at last resolved, it was quickly replaced by a lesser one: the Americans were determined to supplement the cross-Channel landings with a diversion of some of the forces in Italy to an invasion in the south of France, whereas Churchill would have much preferred to mop up the Germans in Italy (where they were still fighting hard) and then drive toward Venice and the Balkans. This time, the Americans got their way. The south of

France operation was itself a success. Although not achieving much in a general strategic context, the decision foreshadowed 1945 disputes by allowing, even encouraging, the Russians to come very far west in Central Europe. On the major issue, Churchill, accepting that 1944 had to be the year of the second front, threw himself enthusiastically into its preparation. His activity was such that a less self-assured president than Roosevelt might have resented the asymmetry between the prime minister's constant on-the-spot interference and his own, more detached position, three thousand miles away.

Churchill's interference took the form of regular meetings between himself, the British chiefs of staff, and one or two other ministers, with Eisenhower or his chief staff officer, Walter Bedell Smith, in attendance. Among other subjects dealt with at these meetings were the detailed plans for the artificial "Mulberry" harbors that were such a successful feature of D-day and the follow-up. Churchill also instituted a weekly Downing Street luncheon between himself and General Eisenhower and Bedell Smith. As the appointed day approached, he took increasingly to prowling around the south coast of England, and visiting troops waiting for embarkation. By mid-May, with the invasion planned for June 5 (it was subsequently postponed for twenty-four hours owing to weather conditions), he had persuaded the commander in chief at Dover reluctantly to accept a plan that would allow the prime minister to watch the action landings from a near offshore cruiser. It required the personal (and rather skillful) intervention of King George VI to procure the abandonment of this madcap plan, as it was generally thought to be.

It was another striking example both of Roosevelt's self-confidence and of his sense of proportion that he did not get in the least agitated about all these activities of Churchill's. FDR had obtained his central objective, the launch of a major American-British force in a frontal attack on the enemy's position in the west. He was perfectly content to let others get on with the details, and if this involved Churchill playing at soldiers, an occupation for which Roosevelt had little taste and, given his wheelchair, less capacity, that was perfectly acceptable.

The first forty days of the invasion were frustrating. The Americans were securely ashore on the Cotentin Peninsula and the British in the bay of Arromanches, but there was no sweeping advance. There was a danger of a repeat of the Anzio landing in Italy of four months before. That disappointment was vividly illuminated by Churchill when he said: "I had hoped that we were hurling a wild cat on to the shore, but all we got was a stranded whale." In the Normandy case the whale was much bigger, but the stalemate did not last beyond July 25.

Then the war of movement began. The consequent vindication of the Roosevelt-Marshall determination on a second front over the more hesitant Churchill-Alanbrooke approach was accentuated by the American Twelfth Army under General Omar Bradley getting most of the superficial glory from the advance. Montgomery's 21st Army Group went through punishing and successful fighting around Caen and Falaise to provide a secure hub, rotating on which the Bradley troops were able to cover spectacular distances, sweeping down the Cotentin Peninsula and then doing a right swing that took them within three weeks to Dreux, Chartres, and Orléans. Paris was occupied by the Allies on August 24 and Brussels on September 3. After that, in the autumn of 1944 and the winter of 1944–45, the war in the west entered into another difficult phase. It is amazing with what tenacity the Germans at Arnhem, in the Ardennes, and then in the Rhineland fought what, by any objective criteria, had clearly become a losing campaign.

Still, by the end of FDR's twelfth year as president, March 3, 1945, it was plain that Germany's defeat could not be far off. The role of the United States in postwar Germany had been settled for many months, although not to Roosevelt's liking. Characteristically, he had told his military chiefs that he wanted the Americans to occupy a northern zone, with direct access to the sea, but had not bothered to inform the State Department of that fact. The talks had produced a British zone just where Roosevelt wished to be and a landlocked American one that he particularly disliked. But, agreement having been reached by negotiators he had not troubled to instruct, he had no recourse save to acquiesce with reasonably good grace. So he did in 1944. By March of the next year, he was even closer to collapse than Nazi Germany, with even fewer weeks to live.

8

Death on the Verge of Victory

There are two salient questions relating to the last year of Roosevelt's life. The first is how and when he approached the question of a fourth term; the second is when his health began seriously to fail. The earlier question was much less traumatic than had been the third-term decision in 1940. With the United States still at peace, although in a far from peaceful world, the breach of a one-hundred-and-fifty-year-old tradition made 1940 a difficult decision. Not so 1944. Then, with American troops engaged all over the globe, and with the war still far from won, the need for continuity of commander in chief was more obvious. Yet the highly controversial decision to run in 1940 was of great benefit to the world, whereas the relatively uncontroversial one to do so again in 1944 was of distinctly lesser value.

There was little about 1944 to contradict the rule that in the highest offices few people have much to contribute after their tenth or certainly their twelfth year. This rule is sustained by Konrad Adenauer in Germany, by Charles de Gaulle in France, and by Margaret Thatcher in Britain; it applies, with one qualification, even to the great Roosevelt in America. It might have been a misfortune for the world had he died in March 1943 (after ten years) with the war just on the turn, but less would have been lost had he left office in January 1945, when his third term expired, except for the highly fortuitous outcome that neither Harry Truman himself, nor anyone else as good as he proved to be, would have got FDR's place at the top of the ticket in the Democratic National Convention of July 1944.

Less would have been lost, but a new president would inevitably have confronted problems. In the United States, with its separate and competitive institutions sharing one another's powers — Congress, the courts, and the executive — new presidents invariably go through a long transition period of learning on the job about the many aspects of policy they have not previously experienced. Their encounters with new programs and relationships are often flawed. The hazards of transition certainly affected Truman and to some degree would have affected anyone then newly in office. Yet 1945, with the war ending and the postwar world only beginning to be shaped, was more than usual a time when continuity could have been useful and might have made a difference to the outcome of important issues.

While Roosevelt's deteriorating health understandably contributed to the deficiencies of his last year in the presidency, it cannot be said to have been a decisive weakness. It is not to be compared with Woodrow Wilson's situation after his disastrous stroke in 1919. Even apart from the crippling effects of his polio, Roosevelt had rarely enjoyed very good health. His temperament was always more buoyant than his physique. In this respect he was no different from Gladstone, who lived to the age of eighty-eight and who, when not suffering from one of his many ailments, was a paragon of physical as well as intellectual activity, or from Churchill, who lived to the age of ninety, often very unwell, but when not so, and even to some extent when on a sickbed, was full of mental, if not always physical, vigor.

The beginning of Roosevelt's decline came in March 1944. With a bronchial infection and a temperature of 104 degrees, he had little choice but to go for a thorough checkup at the Bethesda Naval Hospital. The results were fairly frightening. The diagnosis was acute bronchitis, cardiac failure of the left ventricle, high blood pressure, breathlessness, and some symptoms of long-term heart disease, all exhibiting themselves in a bad gray color and lassitude. The normal semiremedies of a couple of weeks in bed, a sharp weight reduction (he weighed only 188 pounds, but because of his withered legs this was concentrated in his chest and abdomen), and much sedation were rejected on the ground that they could not be reconciled with the president's duties. Eventually it was agreed that he would take digitalis, cut back his smoking to six cigarettes a day, eat less, and take a short, sharp bout of exercise after lunch. He did as he was told, but never asked a question. Perhaps he did not want to know; perhaps he trusted fate, or God; perhaps he did not care.

The physician who carried out the examination was a youngish lieutenant commander in the U.S. Navy Medical Corps named Howard G. Bruenn. Subsequently he visited Roosevelt three or four times a week, and when the president took a two-week holiday at Bernard

Baruch's South Carolina estate, Bruenn went with him. This was as well, for Roosevelt's regular doctor, Ross T. McIntire, did not quite match the admiral's rings on his sleeve with prescience. Bruenn, less casual, was struck by the president's lassitude during the South Carolina visit. Most of the time he just sat, neither working nor reading nor even playing with his stamp collection. And understandably, Morgenthau, the Cabinet officer who knew Roosevelt much the best, was equally shocked by his behavior back in Washington at a Cabinet meeting on March 18, when he displayed an unusual lack of both application and information.

Although only sixty-two, Roosevelt was therefore more or less an invalid for the last year of his life. Nevertheless, he did not seriously consider declining a fourth term. His attention was much more on who his running mate should be. There was general agreement that Henry Wallace would not do; FDR thought he would cut a million off the Democratic vote, and Harold Ickes, never one to be outdone in criticism of others, thought it would be three million. Roosevelt pursued a policy of extraordinary ambiguity, even by his own standards, toward the choice of vice president. Perhaps he thought that with his own nomination a foregone conclusion — he did not even trouble to attend the Democratic convention in Chicago — some tension of uncertainty was needed to keep up the delegates' spirits. The only approach to a revolt at Chicago came from Texas, where Jesse Jones, the secretary of commerce until the election, but not after it, organized a right-wing resistance, of which almost the only effect was to eliminate Sam Rayburn, the majority leader in the House and a liberal Texas congressman, as a serious vice presidential candidate on the ground that he could not even carry his own state delegation.

As late as July 14, Roosevelt wrote a letter for public consideration which was a masterpiece of dissimulation. He said that Wallace was his personal friend (which was very doubtfully true in any except the broadest political sense) and that "I personally would vote for his renomination if I was a delegate to the convention," but he refrained from a full endorsement, which he could easily have enforced, and merely urged the convention carefully to weigh the "pros and cons of its choice." Then he scribbled a note that was claimed to have been seen in two separate versions. The first said that he "should of course be happy to run with either of them [Justice William O. Douglas or Senator Harry S Truman]," while the second reversed the order of those names, and such was the delicacy of the balance that this point assumed a crucial importance. It was like seeing whether a holy relic twitches the right number of times.

Nor was that the end of the complications. James Byrnes had believed that he had been Roosevelt's favorite, and found this letter in either version deeply disappointing. At Roosevelt's behest, he had left the Supreme Court to serve in the White House as director of war mobilization, lifting from the president's shoulders the burden of decision on disputes among the wartime wage, price, and production agencies, and the military services. Byrnes had done an effective job and hoped for a commensurate reward. He reacted with direct courage to the news of Roosevelt's note, telephoned him at Hyde Park, and in his own version — but there is no strong rival one — got the reply "Jimmy, that is all wrong. That is not what I told them. It is what they told me. They asked if I would object to Truman and Douglas and I said no. That is different from using the word 'prefer.' " Byrnes thought that at the end of the call FDR was still urging him to run.

To add to the opéra bouffe element, Truman was by no means clear at this stage either that he was the favored candidate or that he wanted the job. He talked about the historical obscurity that had absorbed so many vice presidents. He must, however, have been aware, perhaps even more than Roosevelt himself was, that on this occasion, if he was chosen, the likelihood was that at some time within the four years, he would become president. Even that did not greatly attract Truman. "I'd rather not move in through the back door," he is recorded as saying. When he left Independence, Missouri, to drive the 350 miles to Chicago (typically, in his own fairly modest sedan, with his wife and daughter), he thought he was committed to making the nomination speech for Byrnes, and was fending off a similar request from Barkley on the ground of this prior undertaking.

When he got to the convention, Truman discovered that Byrnes did not really have presidential backing, that without it he had no strength, but that the pressure was heavily on him, Truman, to let his own name go forward. The pressure came mainly from the political professionals, on whom, with Farley alienated, Roosevelt mostly relied, but when at last forced off the fence, the president himself also pressed. He had been persuaded not only that the party machine would not have Wallace but also that the labor leadership would not have Byrnes. Neither group objected to Truman. Besides, he was the candidate of Robert Hannegan, the Democratic party chairman, also from Missouri, who pushed especially hard. And Roosevelt probably got what he most wanted. Truman's reasonable reaction was, "Why the hell didn't he tell me in the first place?"

The truth was that Roosevelt, although satisfied with the Truman nomination, did not set much store by vice presidents. This had been true with both Garner and Wallace, to different degrees, and the fact that the post, this time, might be of another order of significance did not greatly shift the president's attitude. His combination of optimism and self-confidence must have inhibited him from peering into a future from which he might be absent. He saw Truman only once alone between their joint nominations and the election, with another solitary occasion in the seventy-six days between the election and inauguration; he never saw him at all, except in collective meetings, during the eighty-two days when Truman was vice president.

What, however, was indisputably the case was that Roosevelt, in spite of his health, decided much more quickly and easily than in 1940 that he wanted to run and to win the war. Having so decided, he was determined to win, which was by no means the foregone conclusion in the summer of 1944 that it turned out to be on the night of November 5. An early July poll showed Roosevelt leading Dewey by a margin of only two points: 51 to 49.

So Roosevelt launched an increasingly active campaign, with four main components. First came emphasis on the experienced war leader, the commander in chief, above partisan politics, appealing to swing voters and to movable Republicans. Instead of attending the Chicago convention, the president entrained for San Diego, thence went by sea to Honolulu, inspecting military facilities and conferring with senior officers on the Pacific war, which almost everyone then thought would last at least until the midpoint of the coming presidential term. This remained Roosevelt's stance until after the formal opening of the campaign in early September. Then, without abandoning his wartime role, he began stressing an appeal to middle-class and trade union supporters, and to minorities, in his Democratic voter coalition. He did so by elaborating in speech after speech an "Economic Bill of Rights" for postwar Americans, which he had outlined to Congress in spare yet generalized prose in his January State of the Union address. He now put it increasingly in more specific terms, sketching or hinting at the measures that would become building blocks for Truman's later (partly unenacted) Fair Deal program. These included measures to sustain full employment (then much in doubt), with governmental plans and funds, as needed, to make "60 million jobs" — a target soon exceeded in the burgeoning postwar years — together with a permanent Fair Employment Practices Commission helping to ensure minority jobs. Also included were measures to spur cheap electricity by replicating the TVA on the Missouri River, along with other measures to ensure employees decent minimum wages, farmers proper price supports, veterans decent housing, seniors decent pensions, and everybody health care on a comprehensive basis, something FDR had long desired but previously had not dared to press (he barely did so now; the pressure was left to Truman, who failed — nobody has succeeded since).

Not accidentally, this Economic Bill of Rights bore a family resemblance to proposals in the British Beveridge Report of the same year. The New Dealers who had urged the one were always great admirers of the Liberal reform tradition in the mother country. Roosevelt now put their proposals forward with an eloquence not to be seen again in the United States, not even in the fruitful years of Lyndon Johnson's Great Society, when far more actually got done than Roosevelt's last Congress even tried to achieve.

The third element in Roosevelt's 1944 campaign evolved as September advanced. It was a strong endeavor to energize his activists, to ensure turnout, to guard against fatigue in the ranks engendered by the sense that he was fatigued too. The high point of this effort was a memorable speech in New York City to the Teamsters Union, where with vigor and high humor he attacked the Republicans for spreading untrue rumors of government corruption. The speech was carried on radio, with its highlights covered in the newsreels, especially the moment when Roosevelt, in rollicking form, spoke with relish of the charge that he'd sent a destroyer back to Alaska, at a cost of $2 million or $20 million, to bring home his Scotch terrier, Fala, who'd allegedly been left behind. Not so, Roosevelt said, no truth in it, and while he himself was philosophical about such a canard, "Fala's Scotch soul was furious. He has not been the same dog since." The crowd in the hall, and later at movie theaters, roared with enjoyment. Republicans responded stiffly that this was no way for a war leader to talk. Perhaps that did cost him some swing votes, but his manifest energy, enthusiasm, and amusement were infectious for his partisans. Sixty years later, Democrats then living were still laughing about Fala.

The fourth and final element in Roosevelt's campaign was an effective effort to spike rumors about his health, hence his capacity to carry on. That was never alluded to directly in his opponent's speeches or his own, but whispers were rife and he knew it. The Teamsters speech played a part in his show of well-being, but the effort culminated in a harder test: early in November he was scheduled to campaign in New York for a full day, driving from place to place in a sort of automotive whistle-stop tour. That day it rained, persistently and heavily. Roosevelt persisted too, and made the whole tour in an open car, rain dripping from his hat, his voice firm, his chin at a jaunty angle. News photographs and newsreels did the rest, belying all the rumors. Five months later he was dead, and that day's effort may have played a part, but no one knew this in November.

On Election Day in 1944, Roosevelt was rewarded with a satisfying win. His popular vote was 25.6 million, to 22 million for Dewey, which translated into an electoral college count of 432 to 99. By the 1940 standard this was adequate, although it fell far short of 1936, the triumph long gone. However, the congressional elections were a disappointment, leaving nominal Democratic majorities in both Houses, but majorities smaller than those of four years before, to say nothing of eight. This meant that actual control was vested, as ever since 1938, in a "conservative" grouping (for domestic purposes) of midwestern Republicans and southern Democrats, tempered only by the tendency of southerners to vote with internationalist Republicans, mostly from the East, in foreign affairs. Those were the twin coalitions Harry

Truman had to face in the postwar's first year and a half, until the 1946 elections solidified them further with the coming of Republican majorities. Death spared FDR Truman's experience.

The war did not stop during the 1944 campaign, nor did Roosevelt's concern about the postwar period, which he expected to encompass the second half of his fourth term and to continue after, carrying his legacy. The Economic Bill of Rights testifies to that concern in domestic affairs. But FDR was equally or more concerned with the prospective settlement in foreign affairs. Reasoning from Woodrow Wilson's failures in 1919–20, which Roosevelt knew from being there, he was eager (indeed, anxious) to see the institutions of the postwar world established, in place, working, before the war's end, not after — while the Allies still had common enemies to fight and Americans were still united in pursuit of victory, with the Senate more than usually amenable to international agreements.

Renewed depression, accompanied by disillusioned isolationism at home and a substantial falling-out among the Big Three abroad, seems to have worried Roosevelt during the fall of 1944, as the European war approached its end. Accordingly he pressed for and applauded the agreements on the World Bank and the International Monetary Fund achieved that year, and worked hard to secure what was for him the keystone of the emergent United Nations treaty, the Security Council with its five permanent members and their vetoes, but also with the right to order use of force, a basic improvement on the League of Nations. Provided that the Big Three stuck together, they could use this instrument to guarantee an ordered world. The UN Charter was to be signed in April 1945, at San Francisco. Roosevelt picked the place and planned to be there.

In mid-September 1944, before the height of the political campaign, the president forsook it to meet Winston Churchill in Quebec, well in advance of their next Tripartite Conference with Joseph Stalin, planned for after Christmas. At Quebec, Roosevelt got Churchill's news that Britain was broke and would need an infusion of some $6 billion after the Nazi surrender. The president took that aboard, appearing to believe he owed it to the British, but with no conclusions on how it would be done. Churchill hoped Lend-Lease could be the vehicle, and FDR apparently thought well of the idea. Some of the program's administrators subsequently claimed he'd so decided. Churchill also sought assurance that U.S.-British wartime partnership in atomic energy development would continue after the war. No one then knew if the crash program to develop atomic weapons would succeed before the war's end, but both these men — who themselves had launched that program — apparently assumed it might, some time or other, with domestic energy spin-offs to follow, and Roosevelt readily acceded to continued cooperation (a decision Truman would reverse in relative ignorance eleven months later).

Those were major matters, but this Quebec Conference is best known for something else, Roosevelt's temporary approval of the so-called Morgenthau Plan for postwar Germany, named for its sponsor and promoter, Roosevelt's secretary of the treasury and his neighbor at his mother's place near Hyde Park. The scheme envisaged returning Germany to its pastoral condition before 1870, eliminating industry by sending everything removable to Russia as reparations. The industrial base from which first Wilhelm II, then Hitler had come close to dominating Europe thus would be eliminated for all time. The American army hated the idea, since it then would have to occupy a country without the resources to reconstruct and sustain itself or grow thereafter. The State Department felt no less strongly that the German industrial base was necessary to the reconstruction and growth of all Western and Central Europe. Most British officials agreed. Yet Roosevelt initialed Morgenthau's plan and even got Churchill to do likewise. Churchill's reasons are readily inferred, since he just then was asking for money, and also may have thought of Germans as competitors for British trade. Still, he hastened to dilute his agreement thereafter. But what possessed Roosevelt?

The answer seems to be a combination of tiredness and inattention, exacerbated by poor health, along with genuine liking for the Germany he'd known as a boy and deep repugnance for what Germany had become: all this topped off by the sense that this time, in contrast to 1918, something must be done to spare the world another recrudescence of German aggression. Add some genuine feeling for Morgenthau, who had been loyal to FDR through three terms. If this does not appear a strong, coherent explanation, that also can be gleaned from the haste with which Roosevelt backtracked once his other advisers got at him. By the time he died six months later, he had quietly sabotaged Morgenthau's plan, although under Truman two years would pass before all traces of it disappeared from military policies for occupying the American zone of Germany.

Once the November election was over, Roosevelt turned most of his remaining energy into preparing for the conference with Stalin, now set for February at Yalta in the Crimea. The last German offensive of the war, aimed at Antwerp and culminating in the Battle of the Bulge, determined that the Western Allies would not get as far east before they met the Russians as they once had hoped, but FDR and those around him evidently took this to be no more than a minor setback. Yalta was seen to be the culminating session of the Big Three, face-to-face, before the Nazis were finished.

Many things required to be settled or confirmed or at least raised: the nature of the government of Poland, which the Soviets were just then fully occupying, and its effective borders; the fates of Hungary and of the Balkan countries (except for Greece), also coming under Soviet occupation; the likely locus and procedures for the peaceful juncture of the Allied armies, and their subsequent adjustment to the already agreed zones of military occupation; the character of reparations; renewal of demands for unconditional German surrender; and Soviet receptivity thereafter to joining in the war against Japan, something for which American commanders in the Pacific clamored, especially General MacArthur. Roosevelt also saw the conference as his chance to pin Stalin down to membership in the UN and its Security Council, alongside the United States, before the German war was won.

Since the president's route to Yalta lay near the Middle East, Roosevelt was persuaded of the usefulness of stopping off for lunch on the way back with Ibn Saud, the king of Saudi Arabia, who sat on oil reserves enormously admired by the U.S. Navy. FDR would thus become the first but not the last president to court the Saudis.

Roosevelt spent most of December and January reviewing the proposals and reports of his officials, aides, and diplomats, as well as less formal sources, on all those subjects. Those were the months ordinarily devoted to, among other things, presidential review and presentation of the annual federal budget, but this year Roosevelt secretly delegated all his decisions to his trusted budget director. He also eased his way by truncating the usual inauguration ceremony on January 20, 1945, the start of his new term. Instead of swearing in at the Capitol, before a huge crowd, followed by a long inaugural parade and then by inaugural balls, Roosevelt prescribed a brief ceremony on the White House balcony, followed by a short reception for the relatively few invited guests. The public was told that this was in aid of the war and did not seem to mind. Besides, it rained. In his biography of Truman, Roy Jenkins sketched the scene:

> Roosevelt had done it too often before to be much interested. He made a fairly perfunctory address to the 7,800 [guests], a high proportion from Missouri (one of his few signs of consideration for Truman) who were given the privilege of standing on a squelching lawn, and then [FDR] quickly disappeared upstairs, leaving Mrs. Roosevelt and the Trumans to receive their guests

in their damp shoes and somewhat lowered spirits.

Two days later, the president slipped out of Washington and boarded a cruiser for the first leg of his long trip to Crimea. When he returned after a month's absence, and reported results to Congress (seated as he did so, for the first time in his presidency), the initial response was very favorable. But in subsequent years, as the Cold War became a crucial fact of life, Roosevelt would be more criticized for his performance at Yalta than for almost anything else in his twelve years as president. It was said, especially by Republicans, that he had given away Poland to the Communists, the Baltic states and the Balkans too, trading all these for Soviet membership in the UN and for the hope of Soviet entry into the Pacific war, something not, in the event, actually needed. It was also said that FDR had foolishly or heedlessly played up to Stalin at Churchill's expense, indulging himself in the unrealistic notion that he was a natural mediator between them — but between triumphant Russians and bankrupt Britishers, what meaning had mediation?

On a more detached view, such strictures deserve modification in at least two respects. First, FDR and Churchill "gave" Stalin nothing that he did not actually possess already by military occupation, something they regretted, Churchill especially, but as a practical matter could not reverse. On Poland, in particular, they championed the London government, which had held out there through the war, as the genuine successor to the regime France and Britain had guaranteed in 1939, and indeed had gone to war to support. But the Russians were installing in Warsaw a Lublin government, so-called, consisting solely of Moscow-trained Communists and subordinated Socialists, none of whom had any links to London. At Yalta, Roosevelt and Churchill managed to obtain a Soviet pledge to merge the two Polish governments pending free elections. The pledge was only words, of course, and subsequent Soviet actions belied them as Washington and London understood them.

But second, words had the use for FDR that they enabled him to put the USSR's behavior as an ally to the test of actual performance, not in a military context but rather in the context of political agreements even where the Russians held material advantages. Inevitably, that would often be the postwar context.

So the president saw Yalta as a test of Soviet intent to preserve Big Three comity after the war, thereby bolstering his hopes for the UN Security Council and a peaceful world. According to Charles Bohlen, the Foreign Service officer who interpreted for Roosevelt at Yalta, the president was acutely conscious of Yalta as this sort of test, and quite aware that if the Soviets failed it he would have to face the prospect of something very like the Cold War that actually transpired. This Roosevelt thought it was imperative to avoid if he could, for the sake of the world. So Bohlen told Richard Neustadt in a long conversation five years later, during the Korean War.

By late March 1945, Bohlen added, Roosevelt thought Moscow was failing the test, as Soviet intransigence over the Lublin Poles continued. Had Roosevelt returned to Washington in April, Bohlen believed, he would have joined with Churchill in agreeing to use their military presence on the Elbe and close to Prague as a challenge, confronting Stalin and refusing to withdraw to their previously agreed zones of occupation until he honored their interpretation of the Yalta terms for Poland's government. Roosevelt was already set to go to London with his wife in May, as soon as the Germans surrendered, to visit the king and queen, who had been their guests at Hyde Park just before the war. Bohlen believed that a tripartite emergency meeting, substituted for the later Potsdam Conference, would have followed promptly. Its results, if any, no one can ever know.

Bohlen, incidentally, was probably the last foreign policy specialist to see the president in March, just before he left Washington for the last time. The reason for this is instructive, and sheds light on Roosevelt's administrative instincts and methods. Here he evidently was alert, tired or not, even at the end of his life. Taking advantage of the illness and eventual resignation of Cordell Hull, his longtime secretary of state, with whom he'd never had much temperamental or programmatic affinity, Roosevelt replaced him with Edward Stettinius, a photogenic businessman who had experience of wartime government. Bohlen then was detailed to the president's personal staff with the designation "White House Liaison to the State Department." Obviously, Stettinius was to be a tractable front man, while Bohlen turned selected parts of the department on and off to help the president when he so wished. By various devices, FDR had tried for something of this sort throughout Hull's twelve-year tenure, rarely to his entire satisfaction, never to Hull's. Now, at last, Roosevelt would have it his way. It has often been suggested that he knew he would soon die. Bohlen's appointment belies it.

At the end of March, the president again left the White House for a restful time in Warm Springs, which his intimates hoped would restore his vigor as it had so often before. Indeed, it seemed to do so; the rest was curative and tranquil. On the afternoon of April 12, 1945, he had Lucy Rutherfurd visiting, while a painter worked on a portrait of him and two maiden cousins fussed amiably about. Suddenly Roosevelt complained of a "terrific" headache and then lapsed into a coma. Two hours later, without recovering consciousness, he died — and Truman was president.

As the train bearing FDR's body rolled toward Washington where it would lie in state, respectful mourners lined the tracks. Some scenes were reminiscent of Abraham Lincoln's funeral train in 1865, and foreshadowed Robert Kennedy's in 1968. For, as in those instances, many of the mourners were black. It cannot be said that FDR had singled them out for concern and favor nearly as much as the other men did. But it can be said that what he had done for the aged and unemployed in general, for sharecroppers, trade unionists, and defense workers in particular, and for his countrymen at large, by way of restoring hope — along with all that Eleanor Roosevelt had done in her columns, on her travels, and in entertaining at the White House — had struck chords among black citizens not unlike those the others struck in different times.

The six months after Roosevelt's death offer a wealth of illustrations of that specially American phenomenon of the presidential transition, with associated hazards for new presidents that their experienced predecessors might have handled better. Truman's instincts were to lambaste the Russians over Poland, as he demonstrated when Foreign Minister Vyacheslav Molotov stopped in for a courtesy call en route to San Francisco. But then inherited advisers rushed to say "the boss" had been determined on forbearance, and that Truman should change his tone. Bohlen was not there to rush, having automatically been sent back to the Foreign Service. Nor was Harry Hopkins, then in hospital. Instead Truman heard from Admiral Leahy, who had the imposing title of chief of staff to the commander in chief. The new president took the title at face value, not knowing that Leahy's use to FDR had been mainly as a messenger boy to the military services and as purveyor of their gossip back to him. Truman also took advice from the new secretary of state, who knew only what his officials told him, and from the venerable secretary of war, Henry Stimson, who was out of date on Roosevelt's own evolving views. The president sought advice as well from Jimmy Byrnes, the man he meant to make his secretary of state and shortly did, in part because Roosevelt had taken him to Yalta (as a sort of consolation prize for losing out on the vice presidency). But Byrnes had little background in foreign affairs and anyway knew less than he assumed he did about crucial conversations at Yalta (from which he had been excluded).

We cannot know what FDR might have done in Truman's place about the Polish question, or about the issues that would soon arise of canceling Lend-Lease shipments to the Russians immediately after the German surrender while continuing them to the British solely for the purposes of warfare against Japan. Nor can we know how Roosevelt would have received and thought about the successful testing of a nuclear weapon at Alamogordo in June, or about mounting evidence that the Japanese were concentrating such forces on Honshu that invasion of the island might have to be postponed from November 1945 to March 1946, rendering use of the weapon perhaps less immediately urgent than Truman found it. All we do know is that all those things, as well as funds for Churchill and continued nuclear cooperation, were thoroughly familiar to Roosevelt and probably linked in his mind, not in Truman's.

Six months after Roosevelt's death, with both wars over thanks to Japanese surrender a year "early," Truman sent to Congress a message on domestic issues with a twenty-one-point legislative program. Included among those points were all of FDR's economic measures, along with other liberal proposals on resource development and continued price and wage controls through the next year of industrial reconversion from war to peace. By sending up this program, Truman meant to show that he was a true follower of Roosevelt, not the relative conservative he was rumored to be, while setting the agenda of domestic affairs for the first truly peacetime Congress since the fall of France five years before. As a piece of presentation, written, not spoken, with twenty-one points to boot, and no drama attached then or after, the program was a flop. Again there is no knowing what Roosevelt would have done, but on his previous form at least the drama would have differed.

Do such things matter? Thinking about Stalin on the one hand and Congress on the other, could outcomes have been very different, even if details were not the same? Probably not. But changes of detail there surely would have been had Roosevelt lived another year, and cumulatively this might have made it easier, in a shorter time, with lesser side effects, to turn the country from hot war to cold, as Stalin's further behavior came to compel. The largest, most severe side effect was the McCarthyism of the early 1950s, fueled by the Korean War, which itself had the further, vastly expensive effect of militarizing the Cold War. But by then Roosevelt, had he lived to serve his term, would have been out of office for well over a year. The details that might have mattered long precede that. They, rather, form a cluster around the Polish settlement, the termination of Lend-Lease, the atomic bomb, the British loan, and nuclear collaboration, and in domestic affairs the postwar congressional agenda. Some would add the great prestige that Roosevelt could have had after the war's end and that Truman did not. But recalling how high Wilson's was in 1918, and how fast it fell thereafter, we shall let that pass.

There remains American acquiescence as the British ferried French troops back to Indochina after the end of the Pacific war. This Roosevelt had told his military chiefs to block, knowing that the French lacked ships and sure in his own mind that they had forfeited their right to the region by tamely approving Japanese occupation after their own surrender to Hitler in 1940. (Roosevelt was a confirmed anticolonialist, and wished the British out of India, too.) But the chiefs did not grasp his reasoning and after Japan's surrender interposed no objection to France's return. Truman, knowing little or nothing of his predecessor's views on the subject, did not try to enforce them. To be sure, Ho Chi Minh, the self-proclaimed new head of Vietnam, would have taken the country in a Communist direction, but he was as much a nationalist in Asia as Tito in Europe, and America would probably have got along as well with the one as with the other. Thirty years of tragedy might thus have been avoided.

With more than half a century's perspective, it is evident that Roosevelt made a deep dent on his times; another six months or so might have made the dent a bit deeper. Regardless, from our long perspective one thing seems very clear: the Big Three of the Second World War stand very differently in history. The world we now live in is not Churchill's, with its vanished British Empire, and not Stalin's, with his Soviet Union but a memory, his tyranny fully exposed, and Communist parties dethroned save in Cuba, or immensely reshaped as in China. The world we live in is still Franklin Roosevelt's world, more fragmented yet with population doubled, weapons and communications revolutionized, dangerous in new ways, but essentially recognizable. For good or ill, the United States is at its center, as it came to be in his time, and the presidency is at the center of its government, a position he restored and fostered. His story and he remain vital to the darkened future.

Milestones

1882	Born on January 30 in Hyde Park, New York
1900	Graduates Groton and enrolls at Harvard College
1904	Graduation from Harvard
1905	Marries Eleanor Roosevelt on March 17
1907	Graduation from Columbia Law School
1910	Elected to state senate, representing Dutchess County
1912	Woodrow Wilson elected president, defeating Theodore Roosevelt and William Howard Taft
1913	Appointed assistant secretary of the navy
1914	World War I begins in Europe
1917	United States enters World War I
1918	Armistice ends World War I
1920	Selected as the Democratic vice presidential candidate under James M. Cox; ticket loses to Warren Harding and Calvin Coolidge

1921	Stricken with infantile paralysis (polio) at Campobello Island
1924	Makes first public appearance at Democratic National Convention in New York, nominating Alfred E. Smith as "the happy warrior"
1928	Wins election as governor of New York
1929	Stock market crash; beginning of the Great Depression
1930	Reelected governor of New York in a landslide
1932	Elected president of the United States
1933	Beginning of the New Deal with the "first hundred days" and the creation of the CCC, AAA, TVA, NRA, and other "alphabet soup" agencies; in Germany Adolf Hitler becomes chancellor
1934	SEC created to protect investors and to clean up the securities market
1935	Enactment of Social Security, National Labor Relations (Wagner) Act, WPA; NRA struck down by the Supreme Court; Neutrality Act calls for arms embargo in case of foreign

war; Huey Long assassinated

1936   FDR elected to second term, carrying forty-six out of forty-eight states; Supreme Court continues assault, striking down AAA and other New Deal laws

1937   FDR defeated in effort to "pack" the Supreme Court; delivers "quarantine" speech

1938   Munich conference tests appeasement policy; FDR's "purge" of conservative Democrats fails

1939   Hitler's invasion of Czechoslovakia marks bankruptcy of appeasement; Hitler-Stalin pact; invasion of Poland sets off Second World War

1940   Roosevelt decides to run again; Churchill becomes British prime minister; Hitler's blitzkrieg sweeps through the Low Countries and France; Battle of Britain; Roosevelt elected for unprecedented third term

1941   FDR sets forth Four Freedoms; Congress enacts Lend-Lease; bitter national debate between isolationists and interventionists; Hitler invades Soviet Union;

Roosevelt and Churchill promulgate the Atlantic Charter; Japan attacks Pearl Harbor

1942   "Europe first" strategy via North Africa and Italy; Battle of Midway cripples Japanese sea power; Manhattan Project established for atomic-bomb research and development

1943   Roosevelt and Churchill meet at Casablanca; they meet with Stalin in Teheran

1944   D-day in Europe; American forces recapture the Philippines; plans for the United Nations developed at Dumbarton Oaks; Roosevelt elected to a fourth term

1945   Yalta conference; Roosevelt dies on April 12 in Warm Springs; war ends in Europe; United Nations established in San Francisco; atomic bombs dropped on Hiroshima and Nagasaki bring Pacific war to an end

Selected Bibliography

Acheson, Dean. *Present at the Creation.* New York: W. W. Norton, 1969.

Alsop, Joseph. *FDR: A Centenary Remembrance.* New York: Viking, 1982.

Asbell, Bernard. *The FDR Memoirs.* New York: Doubleday, 1973.

Berlin, Isaiah. *Personal Impressions.* New York: Viking, 1980.

Biddle, Francis. *In Brief Authority.* New York: Doubleday, 1962.

Blum, John M. *From the Morgenthau Diaries.* 3 vols. New York: Houghton Mifflin, 1959–67.

Brinkley, Alan. *The End of Reform: New Deal Liberalism in Recession and War.* New York: Knopf, 1995.

Burns, James MacGregor. *Roosevelt: The Lion and the Fox.* New York: Harcourt Brace, 1956.

———. *Roosevelt: The Soldier of Freedom.* New York: Harcourt Brace, 1970.

Burns, James MacGregor, and Susan Dunn. *The Three Roosevelts: Patrician Leaders Who Transformed America.* New York:

Atlantic Monthly Press, 2001.

Byrnes, James F. *Speaking Frankly.* New York: Harper, 1947.

Cook, Blanche Wiesen. *Eleanor Roosevelt.* 2 vols. New York: Viking, 1992–99.

Dallek, Robert. *Franklin D. Roosevelt and American Foreign Policy, 1932–1945.* New York: Oxford University Press, 1979.

Daniels, Jonathan. *White House Witness.* New York: Doubleday, 1975.

Davis, Kenneth. *FDR.* 5 vols. New York: Random House, 1971–2000.

Eisenhower, Dwight D. *Crusade in Europe.* New York: Doubleday, 1948.

Farley, James A. *Behind the Ballots.* New York: Harcourt Brace, 1938.

———. *Jim Farley's Story.* New York: McGraw-Hill, 1948.

Ferrell, Robert H. *Choosing Truman.* Columbia, Mo.: University of Missouri Press, 1994.

———. *The Dying President.* Columbia, Mo.: University of Missouri Press, 1998.

Flynn, John T. *The Roosevelt Myth.* New York: Devlin-Adair, 1956.

Freidel, Frank. *Franklin D. Roosevelt.* 4 vols. New York: Little, Brown, 1952–73.

———. *Franklin D. Roosevelt: A Rendezvous*

with Destiny. New York: Little, Brown, 1990.

Gaddis, John Lewis. *The Long Peace.* New York: Oxford University Press, 1987.

———. *We Now Know.* New York: Oxford University Press, 1997.

Goodwin, Doris Kearns. *No Ordinary Time.* New York: Simon & Schuster, 1994.

Gunther, John. *Roosevelt in Retrospect.* New York: Harper, 1950.

Hamby, Alonzo. *Man of the People: A Life of Harry S. Truman.* New York: Oxford University Press, 1995.

Hull, Cordell. *Memoirs.* 2 vols. New York: Macmillan, 1948.

Ickes, Harold. *Secret Diary.* 3 vols. New York: Simon & Schuster, 1953–54.

Kimball, Warren F., ed. *Churchill and Roosevelt: The Complete Correspondence.* 3 vols. Princeton, N.J.: Princeton University Press, 1984.

———. *Forged in War.* New York: Morrow, 1997.

Lash, Joseph P. *Eleanor and Franklin.* New York: W. W. Norton, 1971.

———. *Life Was Meant to Be Lived: A Centenary Portrait of Eleanor Roosevelt.* New York: W. W. Norton, 1984.

———. *Roosevelt and Churchill, 1939–1942.*

New York: W. W. Norton, 1976.

Leuchtenburg, William. *Franklin D. Roosevelt and the New Deal*. New York: Harper, 1960.

————. *In the Shadow of FDR*. Ithaca, N.Y.: Cornell University Press, 2001.

Mackenzie, Compton. *Mr. Roosevelt*. New York: E. P. Dutton, 1944.

Moley, Raymond. *After Seven Years*. New York: Harper, 1939.

Morgan, Ted. *FDR: A Biography*. New York: Simon & Schuster, 1985.

Perkins, Frances. *The Roosevelt I Knew*. New York: Viking, 1946.

Roosevelt, Eleanor. *This I Remember*. New York: Harper, 1949.

Roosevelt, Franklin D. *His Personal Letters*. Ed. Elliott Roosevelt and Joseph P. Lash. 4 vols. New York: Duell, Sloan and Pierce, 1947–50.

————. *Public Papers and Addresses*. Ed. Samuel I. Rosenman. 13 vols. New York: Harper; Random House, 1938–50.

Roosevelt, James, and Sidney Shallet. *Affectionately, F.D.R.* New York: Harcourt Brace, 1959.

Rosenman, Samuel I. *Working with Roosevelt*. New York: Harper, 1952.

Schlesinger, Arthur M., Jr. *The Age of*

Roosevelt. 3 vols. Boston: Houghton Miflin, 1957–60.

Sherwood, Robert E. *Roosevelt and Hopkins.* New York: Harper, 1948.

Stimson, Henry L. *On Active Service.* New York: Harper, 1947.

Tugwell, G. Rexford. *The Democratic Roosevelt.* New York: Doubleday, 1957.

————. *In Search of Roosevelt.* Cambridge, Mass.: Harvard University Press, 1972.

Tully, Grace. *F.D.R., My Boss.* New York: Scribner, 1949.

Ward, Geoffrey. *Before the Trumpet: Young Franklin Roosevelt.* New York: Harper, 1969.

————. *A First-Class Temperament: The Emergence of Franklin Roosevelt.* New York: Harper, 1989.

About the Author

ROY JENKINS was the author of twenty-one books, including the *New York Times* bestsellers *Churchill* and *Gladstone*, the latter of which won the Whitbread Prize for Biography. Active in British politics for half a century, he entered the House of Commons as a Labour member in 1948 and subsequently served as minister of aviation, home secretary, and chancellor of the Exchequer. From 1977 to 1981 he was president of the European Commission. In 1982 he became leader of a new party, the Social Democrats, which subsequently merged with the Liberal party to form the Liberal Democrats. In 1987 he became chancellor of Oxford University and took his seat in the House of Lords as Lord Jenkins of Hillhead. He also served as president of the Royal Society of Literature. He died in January 2003.

About the Editor

ARTHUR M. SCHLESINGER, JR. is the preeminent political historian of our time. The recipient of two Pulitzer Prizes and a National Humanities Medal, he published the first volume of his autobiography, *A Life in the Twentieth Century*, in 2000.